third
edition

3

Relationships
FIRST

The New Relationship Paradigm in Contracting
With an Effective Approach to Implementing ISO44001

ANDY AKROUCHE

Motivated Publishing
STUDIOS

Relationships
FIRST

By: Andy Akrouche

Published by: Andy Akrouche
with

Motivated Publishing
STUDIOS

relationships@srscan.com

ISBN (soft cover): 978-0-9919587-2-6
ISBN (eBook):   978-0-9919587-3-3

Printed in the USA

First Edition, May 2013
Second Edition, January 2015
Third Edition, August 2017

Edited by: Beth Parker
Proofreading by: Geri Savits-Fine
Interior layout & Cover design by: Motivated Publishing Studios

The following proprietary tools and frameworks have been developed specifically by Strategic Relationship Solutions Inc.

Benefits Realization Factors (BRF™)

Joint Governance, Accountability and Performance Management framework (GAPM™)

Futuresourcing™

The SRS Relationship Charter or the Relationship Charter

The Rational Model™ (full name, the SRS Relational Business Model™, or the SRS Relational Outsourcing Model™)

For my father...

Table of Contents

Acknowledgements

As is the case with any life journey—whether professional or otherwise—there are many people along the way that made the arrival at the present point in time possible.

For me, the following people (in no particular order of importance), played an important role in the evolution of the model referenced in this book.

Gary Moore, **Raymond Piccard**, Ian Mack, Jon Hansen, Leslie Johnson, Moe Aboufares, Normand Labarre, Peter Bruce, Robert Nadeau, Maurice Chenier, Sam Erry, Scott Leslie, Guy Laflamme and Terry Kulka.

Then there are my family members who helped me tremendously throughout the process: my spouse and partner Aisha as well as my five children Nabila, Adreece, Issac, Jebreiel and Eesa.

Preface

One might reasonably conclude that a book entitled *The New Relationship Paradigm in Contract Management* is an academic text about how to implement the latest collaborative or relational governance models for complex contracting.

While this book does provide instructions and guidance that help organizations source and manage relationships more productively, in truth, this book is an account of my personal, and professional journey.

Over the past 25 years, I have held senior positions with some of the world's largest IT and electronic publishing organizations, including IBM and Electronic Data Systems (EDS). In 1993, I pioneered a new approach to relational governance, which eventually became known as the SRS Relational Contracting and Business Model™ (the Relational Model™).

At the time, my vision for the Relational Model™ was that it would provide a viable alternative within the adversarial world of contract-oriented governance. This model was (and remains today) an innovative framework for structuring and managing business relationships based on strategic fit, flexibility, continuous alignment and sustained mutual benefit.

In truth, these tenets of success are not new. Similar to the principles that define the *Six Sigma Business Management Strategy*, I have built the Relational Business Model™ structure around the enduring core values exemplified by the integrity of intent and mutual or shared partner benefit. Unlike the *Six Sigma*, however, the Relational Model™ has evolved under a "single" architect.

As that architect, I have been in the unique position to chart the evolution of the Relational Business Model™ over the past two-plus decades and its ongoing acceptance and utilization by the public and private sector organizations referenced at length in this book. When I refer to acceptance, this includes the establishment of the new ISO 44001 standard. I will be discussing ISO 44001 at some length in this latest edition.

So why did I write this book?

My primary goal was to provide organizations with a solid and proven framework that can be used to structure (or restructure) the static elements, which have traditionally defined complex contracts and business arrangements.

However, this book is much more than a simple primer.

By sharing my real-life experiences with clients who have played a role in helping the Relational Business Model™ advance over the years, I can provide an honest and meaningful picture of the possibilities provided by this new and emerging relational contracting paradigm.

Although this book is a personal account, I am confident that it will help organizations identify with and better understand the fundamental tenants of the Relational Business Model™ so they can implement it on a level that is most relevant to their organization's unique situations and circumstances.

Section I

The Timeline for Transformation Begins

"Time has been transformed, and we have changed; it has advanced and set us in motion; it has unveiled its face, inspiring us with bewilderment and exhilaration." ~ Khalil Gibran

The SRS Relational Contracting Model (the Relational Business Model™) has evolved through three distinct phases over the past two decades.

The chart on the following page provides an overview of the evolution of the Relational Business Model™ from 1993 into its present form by referencing key accounts that acted as catalysts for innovation. However, it is the form of this innovation (especially as it relates to the challenges and needs of actual clients), which is the real story behind the model's success.

It is no small irony that, like the core of the *Six Sigma* approach (which had its genesis in the 1970s at Motorola as a result of senior executive Art Sundry's criticism of Motorola's poor quality), the Relational Business Model™ was initially developed to address the challenges associated with static contract governance.

In this way, one could view the Relational Model™ as the *Six Sigma* of "effective" relational contracting management principles.

And, like the work of Six Sigma pioneers such as Shewhart, Deming, Juran, Crosby, Ishikawa, and Taguchi

2

who progressed this business management strategy, the individuals who adopted and implemented the Relational Business Model™ are also the co-architects in its evolutionary process.

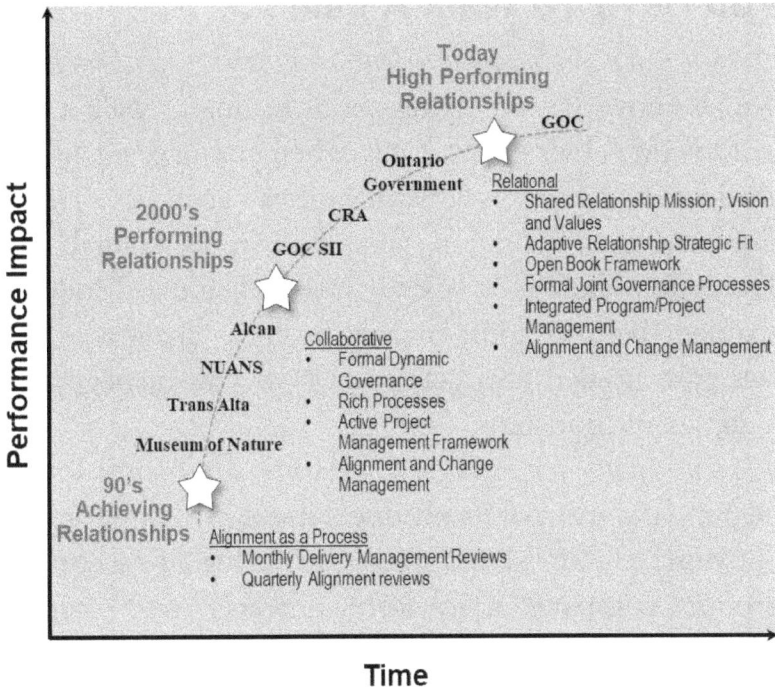

Figure 1: Evolution of the Relational Model™, 1993 - present

I have chosen to begin this book with client stories as opposed to a detailed methodological description. After all, it is the success of these customers that more efficiently speaks to the effectiveness of the Relational Model™, than the mere logic of any instructional text.

Anyone in business can relate to the effort and results of these "diverse" trailblazers and these contextual points of reference.

You Have To Walk A Mile . . .

We all know the old saying about having to walk a mile in someone else's shoes. Only when you understand the challenges faced by organizations such as Digital Equipment Corporation (also known as Digital) and TransAlta, and how using the Relational Model™, enabled them to address their business challenges that you gain needed awareness for how you manage your complex relationships.

Digital, sold most of its products through integrators and outsourcers and was recognized for being an exceptional product company. They were, however, not a service company, nor were they an outsourcing company. Instead, they relied on outsourcing partners who provided services based on the *transformational outsourcing* model of the day.

Structured around three core elements, the Transformational Outsourcing Model effectively implied the following:

1. The vendor takes on existing environment and costs.

2. The vendor transforms environment through leverage, investment in modernization, training and effective management.
3. Costs are much less, and the vendor realizes major savings.

Adopted by public sector organizations such as Canada Post and Ontario Social Services, this approach was the standard of the day during the nineties.

Unfortunately, it was and still is a seriously flawed approach for complex environments. The reason that this was flawed is that even though there was often a burst of initial savings, the client-vendor relationship inevitably failed due to competing agendas. In other words, the vendor's promise of an up-front reduction in operating costs reflected a mindset that said: "let's win the business first and worry about making it work later."

As EDS discovered through a failed major outsourcing contract with the United States Navy in 2000, efforts focused on trying to make the transformational outsourcing model work benefited no one.

EDS was forced to take a first-quarter net loss of $126 million (part of a much larger $334 million write-off). These ongoing and mounting losses were added to a $7 billion multi-year contract to build an intranet for the Navy Marine Corps. Faced with growing economic shortfalls with no apparent end in sight, coupled with pressure from the markets regarding stock prices, EDS had to shift its focus from service delivery to financial recovery.

Unfortunately, during the nineties failed contracts such as this were the norm, and it became increasingly clear that the transformational model did not provide the foundation upon which to build long-term, win-win relationships.

It was evident that something had to change in contracting and contract governance.

The Relational Model™ was the needed change.

chapter 1

The Digital Story

I was working at Digital when I first applied the fundamental tenets of what became the Relational Model™. In 1993, I approached Raymond Picard, the company's chief legal counsel, regarding a new way the company could manage a large IT infrastructure outsourcing contract with the Canadian federal government's Museum of Nature.

Somewhat reluctant at first to make the transition from the "familiar" static contract model, Picard eventually responded well to the idea of testing a flexible agreement with the museum.

Picard and the Museum of Nature's CIO, Normand Labarre, were key contributors to the initial success of the Relational Model™. Picard and I worked together to craft an internally acceptable agreement that would assuage any museum concerns with the new approach.

Labarre then worked with me to put the plan into a public sector contractual framework.

As anyone who has dealt with large government entities will appreciate, cooperation between the vendor and the client was critical in ensuring we received the go ahead. It was also imperative for all of us to fully believe in the model and that it was the ideal framework needed to establish a strategic relationship between the two organizations.

The Need For Champions

On the client side, it is often a single champion who recognizes opportunity and paves the way for positive change. In this case, Labarre, on the client-side, was a key factor to ensure both initial and ongoing success.

Champions are also essential on the vendor side. In this regard, Picard played a significant role. At Digital, Picard's decision to support the undertaking represented a bold move, as it would be considered a departure from the familiar territory (and the false sense of security) that had been at the heart of the belt-and-suspenders type contracts.

It is also I think fair to mention that Labarre's goals were influenced by a pressing need to modernize the museum's technology infrastructure and front office support functions as he was facing severe budget cuts. He believed that this would help the museum to adapt to the many changes it was facing at the time.

Whether you represent the vendor or the client, identifying a champion or champions within all respective organizations is mandatory for success.

Author's Notes

If you are a champion, this book will help you to move forward with the confidence that comes from a proven model. If your champion is another individual within the organization, it is recommended that you share this book with them.

In this case, the ultimate goal was to leverage the organizational structures of both stakeholders (Labarre and Picard) in a way that would maintain a continuing alignment of their respective agendas. This new, collaborative approach ensured that there would be no repeat of the type of disconnect that had plagued EDS and the United States Navy and so many other similar initiatives at the time.

Flying Below The Risk Radar

Ironically, Digital's corporate legal department viewed our negotiated efforts with the museum as being so harmless that they did not even recognize that it was an actual contract. In hindsight, this fact probably worked in our favor because it prevented us from getting bogged down haggling over legal terminology and wording.

Another advantage of being viewed as "harmless", is that the new model was also considered to be a low-risk endeavor.

In retrospect, I am happy that the first introduction of the Relational Model™ was a peaceful one. Unlike the TransAlta case study discussed in the next chapter, where the Relational Model™ experienced a baptism by fire, the Museum of Nature project provided the latitude needed to implement the model without the added pressure of an overly scrutinizing or panicked eye.

Introducing anything new under favorable or relaxed conditions is an important point to keep in mind as you plan how to introduce the Relational Business Model™ within your organization.

Author's Notes

This is an important point to keep in mind as you plan how to introduce the Relational Model™ within your own organization.

My experience with Digital and the Museum of Nature provided me with an opportunity to begin to document the specific processes and factors that would eventually lead to the success of the Relational Model™. By doing so, I recognized early on that stakeholder alignment was the foundation for any and all success in the future.

Key Elements For The Digital–Museum Of Nature Success

In a 2010 blog post ("IACCM's Cummins Hits One Out of the Park Regarding Dishonesty at the Top!," blog post, September 1, 2010), I shared a fascinating exchange between IACCM's founder and CEO, Tim Cummins, and Procurement Insights' Jon Hansen. Specifically (and in response to Jon's position regarding adversarial negotiation tactics) Cummins wrote in his Commitment Matters blog:

"You don't get what you deserve, you get what you negotiate" is the title of a blog by Jon Hansen, in which he challenges the adversarial state of mind ... that for so many years has hindered the buyer and supplier relationship and negatively impacting an organization's ability to sustain positive results.

Jon castigates much of the negotiation training delivered by Karrass and others who encourage the "win-lose" mentality. I agree with his comments. There are still many who see the negotiation itself, rather than the outcome it inspires, as the objective. This transactional, commodity-based thinking certainly does not fit well with many of the relationships required by business today.

Within the article, Jon also addresses the question of "lying" and the sense among many that this is not only acceptable but normal. He suggests such attitudes destroy trust and maintain the cynicism associated with many negotiators, especially those in Procurement.

While broadly agreeing with the point that unprincipled negotiation will lead to disappointing results, I regret that I do not entirely share Jon's perspectives on the question of lying. Sadly, this is not so much to do with the negotiators in sales or procurement—it comes from the top.

I have shared this post because it speaks to the heart of what makes the Relational Model™ successful: *the need for stakeholders to come together in a joint effort to understand and embrace the concept of openness through all phases of the contracting process.*

In other words, it is essential that all contracting parties understand the full implications of doing business with each other: cost, profitability, challenges and current capabilities. To be truly successful, we must abandon the cold war us-against-them mentality and incorporate a relationship-building process into our contracting framework.

Of course, to build such a dynamic and productive relationship requires us to be truthful with one another.

There is no doubt that openness and transparency were the linchpins for the Digital–Museum of Nature success.

The outsourcer and the client management/delivery leads met on an ongoing basis. They conducted a business review of the contract and renegotiated any or all aspects of service including service levels and pricing. Two key processes enshrined in the agreement included a monthly delivery review focused on service-delivery management and a quarterly review focused on IT business alignment.

By providing all stakeholders with ways to adapt to evolving needs, changing market conditions as well as other internal and external factors, we ensured that the contract remained viable for all concerned.

In the Digital–Museum of Nature initiative, stakeholder openness and flexibility were crucial for maintaining a shared agenda as well as achieving mutually beneficial outcomes.

As previously stated, incorporating openness and flexibility is critical to the success of any initiative.

A Word About The Relationship Charter Agreement

The documentation of my experience in establishing a working arrangement between Digital and the Museum of Nature provided the foundational framework for our present day SRS Model Relationship Charter Agreement (Relationship Charter).

The Relationship Charter (covered at length in Section II of this book) is a critical addition to both new and existing contracts.

Unlike the museum agreement that was deemed to be harmless by Digital's corporate legal department, we have come a long way as an industry in recognizing the importance of fully understanding and managing stakeholder relationships.

Also, by coming together under the banner of a shared or mutual objective, we experienced an increase in transparency that bloggers Hansen and Cummins lamented were historically lacking in the buyer–seller relationship.

chapter 2

The TransAlta Crisis: Our First Major Relational Model™ Installation

Sometimes our greatest opportunities are presented to us in the form of a crisis. This perspective was certainly the case in 1994 when Digital's relationship with TransAlta Corporation, Canada's largest publicly traded power generator and marketer of electricity and renewable energy faced a major challenge.

At that time, Gary Moore was appointed CIO for TransAlta. As any new CIO typically does, Moore reviewed the company's progress in achieving its goals and took an inventory of its existing relationships.

Digital had provided service to TransAlta, but after assessing their relationship, Moore felt Digital had consistently failed to deliver on its promise to provide essential services in the areas of data center, help desk, and maintenance support, as well as order management.

Dumped In A Magazine Article

To Digital's surprise and disappointment, Moore shared this revelation in an interview he did for *CFO Magazine*. The article concluded with the comment that TransAlta had decided to drop Digital and was seeking a new supplier.

The TransAlta CIO's public proclamation that Digital would be "dumped" as soon as possible came at a memorable time in my career.

As luck would have it, I was promoted to general manager for Digital's Canadian Operations Management Services a week before the *CFO Magazine* article hit the newsstands. Suddenly, I found myself standing at ground zero of a very public and explosive situation.

Author's Notes

Prior to this promotion, I was in charge of the Eastern Region.

Needless to say, all eyes were on me—even more so after the general manager of the Digital business unit, Tim

Leisman, turned to me at the company's quarterly meeting in Boston and said, "Andy, you've got to fix that."

Talk about a baptism by fire, and it was about to get even hotter!

As with any business arrangement, and especially one where the relationship between the two primary players is already tenuous, an unexpected challenge made the task even more daunting.

For me, this challenge came in the form of Raymond Picard's departure from Digital.

In his role as Digital's chief legal counsel, Picard had played a key role in drafting the agreement with the Museum of Nature, structured as described in the last chapter, around the Relational Model™. Picard had been instrumental in addressing the usual concerns that all lawyers instinctively have with a soft, process-centric approach to contracting.

Now that he was no longer with Digital, I wondered if I would retain the positive inroads I had made in getting the company's legal team on board with the museum initiative.

The prospect of having to start all over again with a new chief legal counsel was daunting, especially at a time when his support would be critical to our success in turning around the TransAlta account.

As anyone in the business world knows, corporate lawyers and the boards they report to have little appetite for entering into relationships without a contract. Given the nature of the relational agreement that Picard had previously authored, in which the usual self-protecting, onerous terminology that is the hallmark of a fixed profit and limited liability "arrangement" was absent, I was concerned that the situation would revert to a battle of terms and conditions as opposed to cooperation and collaboration.

Suffice it to say, if a similar mindset had persisted at Digital, our continuing relationship with TransAlta would have been in real jeopardy. Fortunately, Digital's new chief legal counsel assigned to my business unit, Robert Nadeau, was able to look beyond the usual concerns. Nadeau saw the greater vision and lasting benefits behind my approach.

Over time, Nadeau became such a staunch supporter of the model that he ultimately left Digital to become one of the founding partners of my present-day company, *Strategic Relationship Solutions.* Looking back, I realize that Nadeau's contributions at that critical juncture also made him one of the Relational Model's™ earliest architects.

Having, calmed the internal issues with Nadeau's support, I made a call to Gary Moore. Moore, of course, was already dealing with several pressing issues of his own outside his TransAlta's relationship with Digital.

To start, TransAlta was in the middle of a major SAP implementation. If you have experienced first-hand the challenges and frustrations associated with an ERP (enterprise resource planning) initiative you already know all too well the difficulties this can entail. To further complicate matters, Moore had been asked to respond to concerns regarding the impending Y2K bug.

Known as the *Millennium Bug*, this once-in-a-lifetime problem was the result of abbreviating a four-digit year to two digits. As a result, the British Standards Institute (BSI) had identified two potential problems that existed in the majority of computer programs. The first was the possibility that making the rollover from "99" (as in 1999) to the year 2000 or "00" would lead to logical errors. The second, and lesser known potential problem involved the leap year factor.

As a result of the BSI warning and wide-scale media hype, companies were scrambling to find a resolution to the Y2K problem before the year 2000—which was fast approaching.

In retrospect, many of us are now of the opinion that the Y2K bug was driven more by fear than an actual threat.

All the dire predictions that the world would come to a screeching halt proved to be unfounded. At the time, however, no one anticipated anything other than the worst-case scenarios. As a result, organizations were spending a significant amount of time and resources on addressing the problem.

Rather than being deterred by the whirlwind of circumstances putting everyone on edge, I saw the TransAlta account as a great opportunity. It was a perfect time to expand on the model's application and implement some much-needed change by strengthening our relationship with the company.

Buoyed by this optimism, I called Moore and scheduled a meeting at the head office in Calgary to discuss the nature of the relationship to that point in time.

At that meeting, Moore told me that he was looking for positive changes in several critical areas, including a marked improvement in the level of service Digital was providing to his company. Moore also demanded a significant increase in upfront savings and most importantly, year-over-year savings going forward.

Based on Moore's feedback, I suggested that a Digital team meet directly with TransAlta's end-users. It was through these "workshop-like" meetings that we came to understand the nature of the problems and how we could address Moore's concerns.

It is worth noting that around this time, Moore was also being wined and dined by Digital's competitors: IBM, EDS, and SHL Systemhouse. This level of interest was not surprising. TransAlta was, at the time, one of the biggest and most sought after contracts in the country, generating over $15 million in revenue on an annual basis.

Competition notwithstanding, and armed with the information my team had gathered during our discussions with TransAlta's end-users, I scheduled a follow-up meeting with Moore. It was time to lay my cards on the table.

I acknowledged the areas where we needed to improve and assured him that I would implement the required changes in short order. More importantly, I asked him the following question; "Gary, what will it take to build our relationship?"

You might wonder if this was the right time to be asking such a direct question. However, I have always believed that one of the fundamental tenets for mutually beneficial and enduring relationships is transparency. Despite the industry's contradictory beliefs that "you don't get what you deserve, you get what you negotiate" (see page 11), my approach was to facilitate an exchange that would tell it like it is.

I reminded myself that if it didn't work out, at least I would not have to second-guess myself and regret my lack of openness. So I put it all out there on the table for everyone to see.

To my relief, Moore responded to my question positively, by providing me with an in-depth understanding of his priorities for the organization.

After I had met with Moore, I assembled my team in a hotel room across from the TransAlta head office. For the next two weeks, we worked around the clock to formulate a proposal that would satisfy the company's needs.

Once completed, we developed a short and incredibly simple 20-page agreement which included a set of outcomes and an implementation plan as well as a financial management plan. This new governance agreement provided the framework for us to move forward with TransAlta.

Digital's Board's Buy-In

Before presenting the Agreement to Moore, I had to get the Digital Board of Directors to sign-off on it.
As I alluded to earlier, corporate boards usually do not make a habit of endorsing anything other than what they consider to be an ironclad contract. In the case of

TransAlta, I was lucky that Digital's board was focused more on saving the account than sticking with "boundary-in-the-box" protocol.

I have been asked many times if the sense of urgency to save the TransAlta account contributed to the board's approval of my simple 20-page relationship agreement.

My answer is always the same, probably not. But I do think that, as the saying goes, "Chance favors the prepared mind." In this context, I was definitely in the right place at the right time, with the right approach, both with TransAlta and the earlier referenced Museum of Nature.

Of course, both were key early adopters of the relational model albeit for different reasons.

The museum contract provided the perfect opportunity to test the Relational Model™ in a non-critical environment. With them, the stakes were minimal, especially since I was not being asked to save an account.

Even though my approach with the museum had an adverse impact on my "personal" remuneration package; I saw the account as an important opportunity to change the way in which the company (and eventually the industry) did business. The recognition of this opportunity allowed me to focus on what I call the shared mission approach, which was and remains a fundamental tenet of the Relational Model™ today.

Author's Notes

This was because Digital did not consider it to be a bona fide contract.

I cannot underestimate the importance of this first success with the museum and how it paved the way for the use of the Relational Model™ with TransAlta. I am confident that the earlier success alleviated at least some of the concerns that the Board might have had when I suggested taking the same approach with a major account in crisis. As a result, I was given lots of latitude in my efforts to get the job done with TransAlta.

Needless to say, this simple agreement (now worth $110 million) was ratified by the board.

Of course, when you are under pressure and focused on trying to save a major account, there is not much time to step back and appreciate the magnitude of your journey. It's like climbing Mount Everest. As you ascend the mountain, your attention is focused upwards, and you don't have much opportunity to marvel at the heights you have already scaled. When you finally reach the summit and plant your flag, then and only then do you look down and realize the magnitude of your accomplishment.

The pinnacle of my experience with the TransAlta account took the form of a gift from its CIO, Gary Moore, which still has enormous significance for me.

Moore gave me a flexible cube that allowed me to turn it into the shape of either a pyramid or a sphere or anything in between. This cube symbolized perfectly the flexibility of the Relational Model™ approach to contracting and the shared mission and joint governance that made us all part of the same team.

It was the ideal representation of what I was determined to achieve in our ongoing relationship with TransAlta and all of Digital's other customers.

The fact that Moore had found this cube and equated it with what we were trying to accomplish collectively has remained with me to this day. It was a pivotal moment that for me, solidified the belief that the Relational Model™ was the only way to structure a complex and important business relationship.

Adopting the Relational Model is a recognition that the entire contract is not in the four corners of the agreement document, but will be informed by the relations of the parties and their priorities over time.

Key Elements In Digital's Transalta Success

The Digital and TransAlta teams worked together to formulate a new proposal centered on three key components:

1. Establishing a strategic relationship focused on improving services and generating savings, that both teams believed were achievable. The estimate had an immediate impact that fiscal year laying the foundation for a business process improvement strategy that would generate savings in future years.

2. Creating a governance framework that would manage our relationship on a monthly and ultimately quarterly basis and keep it aligned so that we could each achieve our outcomes. (Note: I attended every review session.)

3. With the TansAlta account, the Relational Model™ was focused initially on the development of a strategic plan for the relationship first and then the establishment of a governance framework or Relationship Charter. We took this approach because we were behind the proverbial eight ball as the relationship was already in trouble. Ideally, the Relationship Charter should be established first as it provides the basis for the development and maintenance of a strategic relationship plan.

It is worth noting that there was very little transparency in the financial management of the TransAlta arrangement. What this meant is that we had a collaborative relationship whereby we worked jointly to achieve our respective financial objectives, without TransAlta being privy to Digital's margins or key internal financial success factors. Today, and through the introduction of the Open Book Framework, complex relationships have a much higher degree of transparency which eliminates the inherent risks that lead to a splintering of agendas. I will talk about this in detail in a later chapter.

chapter 3

The NUANS of a Successful Public-Private Partnership

Following the back-to-back successes with the Museum of Nature and TransAlta, one could safely conclude that we had successfully charted the Relational Model™ course for the future. There is no doubt our achievements had garnered attention as well as added credibility. However, big ships and industries (as the saying goes) turn slowly.

From a personal standpoint, I enjoyed the benefits of these early wins as demonstrated by my promotion to corporate vice president. However, in truth, many believed that my success had more to do with my positive reputation with the Digital corporate office, which had credited my favorable results more to what they called my "winning personality" than to the model itself. While I appreciated the fact that they believed in me and the value I brought to the table, I knew that their confidence in me meant that they were still not convinced that the

Relational Model™ was the harbinger of a new business approach.

A Culture Of Empowerment

Digital was a progressive organization that fostered a culture of empowerment. For this reason, it was the ideal company to introduce and develop the Relational Model™. Because of this, I had the freedom to pursue my vision. I am not confident that I would have had the same latitude and trust with either an EDS or IBM.

The Digital spirit of personal empowerment notwithstanding, I was still required to have all contracts assessed by the company's project approval and review board. This process was by no means easy. Simply put, the board continued to view the management of all agreements through a traditional contracting lens. This mindset meant that there was a continuing dependency on familiar terms and conditions that had always served as guidelines for structuring business arrangements.

Introducing and championing the Relational Model™ placed me in the position of fitting a round peg into a square hole. It meant that I had to be creative in establishing a contextual link that acknowledged the board's comfort level while still meeting the flexibility demands of a real-world client. Finding the balance between these two points of contradiction was at first a challenge, as traditional contracts relied upon a static and inflexible governance model to achieve its objectives.

Conversely, the model I was proposing required active management which was a departure from the sign-and-forget-about-it relationship that usually existed between two separate and distinct entities. In other words, for the Relational Model™ to achieve optimal results, ongoing involvement and a cooperative mindset in which change was embraced rather than legislated or just avoided were required.

In the early to mid-nineties, this approach was not only new; it was revolutionary, bordering on seditious. Negotiating contracts at that time relied upon an onerous push-pull adversarial process, in which each party squared off in a risk-adverse battle of wills.

This approach was not purposefully rooted in a desire to put one over on the other guy as the parties to a contract had every intention of doing a good job and delivering value. They only wanted to do it on their terms and according to their unilateral capabilities and timelines. If something went wrong (as it often does with static governance models), the priority would instantly switch from *ability* to *liability* and from service *intent* to service *defense*.

Under this kind of contracting mentality, it was practically unheard of for two parties to come together under a transparent and collaborative umbrella to deal with challenges and changes on a cooperative basis.

The glaring inefficiencies of this traditional approach are why I first sought to create a viable, real-world alternative that was relationship-driven and based on mutual gain through greater shared flexibility and ongoing dialogue.

Despite the continuing reluctance of the review board to eschew their ingrained contracting principles, the success I experienced through the museum and TransAlta contracts helped me to place a critical stake in the ground. As a result, I was able to introduce the Relational Model™ as a proactive selling tool that could win business rather than simply save accounts.

This crack in the door led to a greater latitude in the review board's attitude towards the new model, and it is reasonable to suggest that my experience with new technology—NUANS was an important tipping point towards mainstream acceptance.

Enter NUANS

The *Newly Updated and Automated Name Search* or NUANS is an intelligent computerized system used to conduct corporate name searches. The primary purpose of NUANS is to enable those making a new name inquiry to determine if there is a potential conflict with an existing company name or trademark.

In 1993, the director of information technology at Industry Canada, Peter Bruce, had just completed the development and testing of NUANS. Bruce had decided to turn to the private sector for additional investment in technology infrastructure and operations management.

In addition to providing the required investment, Bruce hoped that the right private sector partner could improve service quality and availability. He was also looking to this partner to act as the eventual reseller of the NUANS service to Canadians through law firms and other institutions.

Unlike the museum account that had provided a low-key, behind the scenes initiation for the Relational Model™ and the stressful TransAlta crisis, the NUANS partnership introduced a high level of complexity to the relationship management structure. NUANS represented a new test of the model's effectiveness in establishing and managing critical relationships involving multiple partners from both the private and public sectors.

Like the Relational Model™, partnering for NUANS was a new approach that had yet to prove its value. Being "unproven" meant that if we were going to be successful, Digital (and more specifically, my team) would have to facilitate the relationships between Industry Canada and the private sector organizations upon whose shoulders NUANS' success would ultimately rest.

At this point, it is worth noting the emergence of a trend, which would eventually become a significant harbinger of success for the Relational Model™. Although individual client needs and the circumstances under which we introduced the model varied, the vision, leadership and courage of the key organizational players was an important constant in the success of every initiative.

For example, if Bruce had failed to recognize the need to marry public sector "vision" with private sector "execution," NUANS might never have gained the necessary traction to become the universal tool that it is today. Stepping outside of a familiar framework to seek an external partner demonstrated tremendous courage on the part of Bruce.

Author's Notes

Bruce eventually moved on to become the CIO at Agriculture Canada and later, Assistant Deputy Minister at Shared Services Canada.

The same level of courage was also present with Moore, the CIO at TransAlta;, Labarre, the CIO at the Museum of Nature; and the CIO of Alcan Aluminium. I will be discussing the Alcan story in the next chapter.

These individuals' willingness to look beyond familiar and safe arrangements in favor of pursuing a flexible business relationship model epitomizes the true spirit of thinking outside of the box.

The Framework For NUANS' Success

"A cooperative venture between the public and private sectors, built on the expertise of each partner, that best meets clearly defined public needs through the appropriate allocation of resources, risks, and rewards."

The above paragraph is how The Canadian Council for Public-Private Partnerships (CCPPP) defines both the framework and intent of a collaborative partnership between public and private entities.

In 1995, when Industry Canada began looking for a private partner for the NUANS project, the CCPPP (founded the previous year) was still a relatively new organization. For that reason, it is fair to say that the Relational Model™ was a trailblazer in creating a relationship management framework for public and private sector entities.

Today, there are many reasons why a strategic bond between public enterprise and private industry is critical. While there are also many different models used to define the formation and management of a collaborative process between these two distinct sectors, it is safe to say that with the introduction of ISO 44001, the Relational Business Model™ has become the de facto standard for public-private sector relationships management.

The fact that the Industry Canada–Hewlett Packard NUANS relationship is still thriving after all these years gives credence to the veracity of this assertion.

chapter 4

When David Met Goliath— The Alcan Outsourcing Arrangement

Despite the early success of the Relational Model™, both Digital and the industry, in general, remained reluctant to fully embrace a flexible relationship framework as the new standard for managing complex business relationships.

The public sector procurement regime of the day relied on a benefit-driven procurement (BDP) structure, which while focused on testing industry capability to achieve certain outcomes or benefits, had, however, lacked the operational model to facilitate the realization of said benefits.

Specifically, you have a "capability" based RFP process, but you still have the same rigid contractual framework with its transactional orientation within a compliance based oversight management model. In essence, the BDP approach gave little more than a passing acknowledgment to the concept of a truly flexible relationship ideal.

Despite the obvious issues with BDP, some maintained that it was an improvement over its predecessor because of the belief that it facilitated a sharper focus on outcomes vs. process, (the common purpose procurement policy). However, the Museum of Nature and NUANS, let alone TransAlta would never have achieved the same outcomes with a BDP approach without the incorporation of the Relational Business Model™ of Management.

Perhaps this is the reason why the Alcan opportunity became a watershed account in the evolution of the Relational Model™.

I still remember the day I received a call from our Montreal representative who informed me that Alcan was looking to outsource critical functions within its enterprise. He told me that they were going to be holding a bidder's conference and suggested I attend.

When I arrived, I immediately noticed that the meeting included a who's who of the high-tech world. Anderson Consulting was managing the procurement process, and with companies such as IBM, EDS and other notables in the audience, the situation had the air of a major event. Not surprisingly, CGI was there in full force and appeared to be the incumbent vendor.

There was no doubt that in the context of outsourcing, Digital was a "small" David in the midst of a room filled with Goliaths. Those in attendance must have wondered why we (the Digital Outsourcing guys) had even bothered to show up, let alone consider pursuing a business opportunity with another global giant, Alcan. They apparently didn't count on the influence and foresight of Alcan Aluminium's IT and CIO organization's leadership, which had Jacques Bougie at the helm.

The Lay Of The Alcan Landscape

As mentioned in the previous chapter, Alcan was willing to look beyond their familiar, existing relationships to make the right partnering decision to support a major transformation of the company's ERP systems and support services. In retrospect, Alcan's willingness to think outside of the box flew headstrong into the face of the conventional wisdom of the day, which is to go with what you know and are most comfortable. Alcan wasn't looking for comfortable; they were looking for outcomes.

As a small outsourcing group within the Digital organization, no one expected for a moment that we would be a serious contender in the competition for this global contract.

Nevertheless, Digital was the only company that Alcan believed could provide the infrastructure and operational flexibility needed to support a major ERP transformation.

We ultimately emerged as the best bidder by offering Alcan a relationship structure built around an efficient transition management process, and the assurance of ongoing alignment and best pricing. In essence, we offered them a true functioning partnership.

Considering that this was the first time we had responded to an RFP request with the Relational Model™ in the private sector, we did very well. And we did so in direct competition with CGI, which was already the vendor of choice as they had been delivering the data center services and distributed computing services on a global basis.

I have often been asked why, in an era when contract bundling was an accepted practice, that CGI or any of the other big players did not make us a part of their bid response. It does seem odd that these players did not contact us to work with them.

The only answer I can offer is that perhaps it was because the company had not considered the possibility of losing the account to a product company and a much smaller operations management services player.

Regardless of the reason, the biggest lesson I had learned from winning the Alcan contract is this; when faced with the opportunity to enter into a true partnership based on a shared mission and purpose, there is no other alternative. You must choose to collaborate.

The fact that Digital won the contract was a hard pill for CGI to swallow. Even though they maintained a healthy share of Alcan business, our outsourcing win was a major embarrassment. I am sorry to say that on those occasions when our two companies needed to work together within the Alcan account, the CGI team was a bit cold.

Expectation

CLIENT	SERVICE PROVIDER
• Build new product or introduce new enabling technologies	• Profits
• Lower cost, improve lead times	• Leverage existing infrastructure and capabilities
• Increase organizational agility / flexibility	• Transformation of infrastructure & sustainability of compelling value proposition to customers
• Focus on core business, increased productivity	• Increased business volume or market share

Outcomes

Sometime during the term of contract some or all of the following may be experienced:

• Change in product requirements, service definition or demand for product or service

• Change in management – Execs who did the "deal" are no longer around

• Change in business requirements

• Initial vendor operational leverage assumptions are weak. Core assumptions are inaccurate.

• Vendor becomes reliant on change order process. Client becomes hostage of this process

• Expected benefits now appear to be more difficult to harvest than originally expected

• Contract too rigid/inflexible.

Adversarial

Limited Success
Relationship

Figure 2: Client and Service Provider Expectations and Outcomes

So why did Alcan choose Digital? What gave Alcan the confidence to award a major outsourcing contract to a nascent outsourcing organization, one that championed a model most would dismiss in a heartbeat?

It was because Alcan's CIO and IT management group in Canada and the United Kingdom were real leaders. They recognized the importance of relationships.

Alcan also understood the principles (outlined in the slide above), that I had used in my presentation to them. This slide explains the structural issues and fundamental problems associated with a lose-lose relationship.

Despite these significant wins, Alcan's leadership team and the leaders of the other organizations that had chosen to also go with the Relational Model™ approach were "few and far between." Of course, back then, there wasn't an ISO 44001 standard that today recognizes and reflects the fundamental tenets of the relationship model. Knowing that a wider adoption of the Relational Model™ would produce equally impressive results for all organizations, I began the evangelizing process by leaving Digital to start Strategic Relationship Solutions Inc. (SRS).

I reasoned that by assuming the neutral advisory or consultancy position between vendors and the end-user market itself, I would be afforded a greater opportunity to influence executive thinking. Or to put it another way,

I felt the time had come to position myself as working for all parties as opposed to working for a particular vendor.

chapter 5

The Long and Winding Road

"The long and winding road that leads to your door . .
. Will never disappear . . . I've seen that road before,
it always leads me here . . . Leads me to your door."
~ Paul McCartney

As I look back on the early years and my efforts to make a case for the new paradigm represented by the Relational Model™, it has indeed been a long and winding road.

However, as I traveled this road, there was never any doubt in my mind that the model was the right answer and the right fit in many diverse situations. The Relational Model™ remained a constant whether we were putting out a fire with TransAlta or blazing a new trail with Alcan.

The Relational Model™ was a door that opened up a whole new world of possibilities in managing complex relationships.

As the years progressed, the model continued to enjoy repeated success with many public-private relationships, including initiatives involving Revenue Canada, the Ontario Ministry of Government Services, Ministry of Transportation and the Government of Canada.

As interest and word spread about the Model, more people began to pay attention. Included among the growing list of converts were professors and executives-in-residence at Ottawa University's Telfer School of Management. These individuals helped shape some of the tools that we continue to utilize today for sourcing relationships instead of transactions or deals. As a result of their first-hand knowledge and experience with such analytical tools, Telfer proactively sought ways in which they could expand their relationship with my company.

In fact, Telfer's executive director, Doug Dempster made these remarks when the school co-sponsored an SRS seminar on relational outsourcing management in the public sector:

> *"In today's environment, executives and managers face tough outsourcing decisions on a regular basis. Our partnership with SRS is a reflection of our continued commitment to excellence in executive leadership and management training."*

Given this kind of support and the steadily increasing adoption of the Relational Model™, you might think it was time to queue the closing music and roll the credits. The perfect happy ending!

However, making the transition from a rigid performance-based legislative transactional mindset to structuring relationships is a process that is far easier said (or imagined) than done.

Old Habits are Hard to Break

These attributes appear to play a major role in the context of IT outsourcing relationships in that successful management of an outsourcing relationship today requires a highly interactive, flexible relationship between two organizations in order to sustain over the strategic planning horizon. ~ Williamson, O.E. The Role of Service Level Agreements, 1985

Although the above quote may seem obvious, in the procurement world nothing could be further from the truth.

As Williamson pointed out in his 1985 conceptualization of relational governance, it has long been the order of the day to use economic weapons as hostages and commitments to keep opportunistic behavior at bay. In essence, financial inducements such as penalization for missed service level agreements (SLAs) had been considered the only means through which a contractor could ensure vendor performance.

It was not until recently that this "sledge hammer" style of contract management gave way to a more socially oriented enforcement of obligations, promises, and expectations that promote flexibility, solidarity, and information exchange. (Poppo and Zenger, 2002)

When I talk about a socially oriented approach, I am looking at it from the standpoint of creating an environment of trust among the major stakeholders. The resulting trust paves the way for improved communication that will not only recognize and acknowledge problems but provides a mechanism for dealing with them from the outset rather than remaining hidden and festering into siloed agendas of self-interest.

The socially oriented approach, which reflects the core principles or values of the Relational Model™, leads to greater cooperation within a contract's framework by encouraging stakeholders to identify potential problem areas with the intent of reaching mutually beneficial resolutions. The decision to actively seek collaborative solutions to contract challenges is the antithesis of the economic levers associated with traditional contract management methodologies as the latter inadvertently rewards the wrong behavior by punishing disclosure rather than rewarding it. In other words, one is unlikely to admit an error if doing so results in financial retribution.

For example, rather than penalizing a stakeholder for a missed SLA, it would make far more sense to address the issue through a full disclosure and review of the delivery process capability under an umbrella of a Jim Collins autopsy "without blame approach." [xxxii]

In this way, a vendor's ability to effectively communicate and collaborate would be the basis for their selection as a partner. In a complex global marketplace, problems or challenges are a given. Dealing with them as opposed to denying them is a fundamental tenet of the SRS Relational Business Model™.

Despite the obvious need to be relational, buyers often remain reluctant to rely solely on the relational attributes of what *The Role of Service Level Agreements* paper refers to as a trust arrangement. So, while formal contracts often have hindered the meaningful formation of collaborative or relationship-driven interaction, they provide a familiar and therefore comfortable fallback position that can be difficult to relinquish.

"You cannot steal second base with your foot firmly planted on first." ~ Frederick B. Wilcox

Although this fallback tendency is somewhat ingrained, the truth is, if a formal contract hinders the ability for all parties to openly and transparently communicate, then relationships inevitably stagnate and are unlikely to progress to the point that would warrant a non-contractual trust arrangement.

The Relational Model™ Answer

Can a hybrid approach in which you can incorporate some elements of a traditional contract into a relational governance framework succeed?

Not only is the "merging" of the contractual elements within the structure of a relational governance model possible; it is also effective. According to Baker et al. (1994) and Mayer and Argyres (2004)[i] "the process of developing a comprehensive and complex contract requires parties to engage in joint problem-solving." This collaborative approach, in turn, will further enhance the relationship-building process between stakeholders that might not otherwise have been possible.

The obvious key to success is to find the desired and needed balance between contractual imperatives and relational execution. As demonstrated repeatedly, the Relational Model™ is the mechanism or means for achieving this important balance or alignment.

Flexibility as Opposed to Rigidity

Reliance on rigid contract terminology to ensure vendor performance is detrimental to building successful relationships. However, this does not mean that contracts should be eschewed outright.

In the *Role of Service Agreements* paper, Williamson makes the argument that SLAs *can* play a role in "fostering harmonious, cooperative relationships that have high levels of trust and commitment." Included in this is the empirical examination of the specific characteristics of formal contracts that "help in building partnership-style relationships."

Within the framework of the Relational Model™, the alignment concept represents a living document that provides elastic contracting guidelines, which adapt to changing realities or market conditions (including economic circumstance).

The key to accepting Williamson's assertion that contracts can help in building stronger relationships is dependent on the willingness of all parties to no longer rely exclusively on contract terminology to achieve their desired outcomes.

Doesn't Contractual Elasticity Already Exist?

Some have suggested that the mechanism for achieving ongoing adaptability to changing circumstances already exists through the change-order process associated with traditional project management practices.

I disagree with this assessment. Rather than facilitating greater flexibility, the change-order process creates a straight-jacket rigidity that can negatively impact an individual stakeholder and therefore the collective interests of all stakeholders. In other words, the change-order process as we know it creates slaves to rigid contract terminologies that eventually prove ineffective and irrelevant over time.

Not An Either-Or Scenario

"Formal contracts and relational governance function as complements and not as substitutes," (Williamson, 1985)

In the above statement, Williamson reasonably concludes that far from being an either-or situation, there exists within the relational structure a collaborative give-and-take capability that enhances contract performance. However, to get to this point, there has to be a conscious decision to move away from the blind enforcement of dormant terms and conditions that are based more on legal-speak than delivering a practical execution value.

Only when relationships serve as the "lead" metric for both managing and measuring the effectiveness of a contract, will we see an alignment of the three relational governance attributes; relational norms, harmonious conflict resolution, and mutual dependence, with the three "corresponding" SLA characteristics; foundation, change, and governance.

I will talk about governance attributes and SLA characteristics in greater detail in Section II, as well as the emergence of the new ISO 44001 standard.

Section II

A Practical Understanding of the New Paradigm

Referencing Section I, let's review the key elements of the Relational Model™.

Why Do The Majority Of Complex Business Arrangements Fail?

Despite industry's best efforts to modernize and professionalize sourcing practices, project management, and service delivery methods, 70 percent of significant business relationships or large projects do not meet their objectives.

The reason for the high rate of failure is because *organizations in both the public and private sector engage partners based on a static requirement or requirements that are only valid at a "specific" point in time.* Relationships that are structured around this approach inevitably fail because a rigid transactional mindset does not allow for the natural evolution of needs and stakeholder capabilities.

In the case of Futuresourcing™, there is a magnification of the problems as new service requirements mean that the client and vendor are almost always working outside of their experience base. This lack of experience means vendor responses to future-sourcing bid requests are speculative and often tied to a mindset of "let's win the business first and worry about making it work afterward."

As covered in the first Section of this book, the failed relationship between the United States Navy and EDS demonstrates the folly of this approach.

However, and even with the paucity of positive outcomes relative to static and future-sourcing initiatives, the old approach to complex business arrangements continues to be the norm in the industry.

To reverse this trend, we must change our mindset around contracting and contract governance. We have to adopt a relational perspective when seeking and engaging partners.

What Does It Mean to Be Relational?

The Relational Model™ is a viable alternative to the adversarial nature of contract-oriented governance. It represents a new framework for structuring and managing business relationships based on strategic fit, flexibility, continuous alignment and sustained mutual benefit.

At the Centre for Relational Contracting and Strategic Management (for more information visit: http://www. srscan.com) "relational" is defined as a process-centric interaction and a delivery management model that fosters the following:

✓ **Relating** – Connecting and linking in a naturally complementary way.

✓ **Mutuality** – Sharing similar views or outputs.

✓ **Respect** – Recognizing each other's needs, requirements, contributions, abilities, qualities, and achievements.

✓ **Innovation** – Using combined strengths and synergies to deliver improved relationship outcomes.

✓ **Empowerment** – Introducing joint management structures and processes for efficient and timely decision-making within scope and envelopes of authority.

✓ **Continuous Alignment** – Making necessary adjustments and business process improvements to optimize outcomes while maximizing "achievable" benefits.

These tenets of success are not new. Similar to the principles that define the Six Sigma business management strategy, they reflect a structure built around the enduring core values of integrity of intent and mutual or shared partner benefit.

The Relational Model™ Is A New, Socially Oriented Approach

Near the end of Chapter 5 (page 43), Williamson observed that traditional relational governance models, which stressed the use of economic weapons to ensure positive vendor performance gave way to a socially oriented enforcement methodology.

The socially oriented relational approach focuses on creating an environment of trust among the major stakeholders. However, while potential problems can be recognized, acknowledged and dealt with, the absence of appropriate mechanisms means that it ultimately results in little if any meaningful action being taken to remedy the pressing problems of a given situation.

In short, there was a need to move beyond good intentions to a "good" execution of the relational strategy.

The Relational Model™ Is A Proven Approach

The Relational Model™ for complex business arrangements was developed by SRS long before the widespread recognition of Poppo and Zenger's socially-oriented concept.

During the past 20 years, the Relational Model™ has proven its viability in practice through many successful high-profile client successes by focusing on stakeholder relationships as the pivotal point to measure performance, continuous delivery and service management capabilities.

The foundation of the Relational Model™ is a reliance on joint or shared governance and management structures, including the processes to facilitate; collaboration, gain meaningful insight into relationship parameters and to proactively manage collective resources to achieve expected relationship outcomes.

The Relational Business Model™ incorporates the following three elements which are relational contracting, relationships management and collaborative working into a cohesive operational framework to achieve optimum "relationship" performance:

✓ **Relational Contracting** – An industry engagement and partner selection system to ensure alignment with overarching program objectives. Relational Contracting recognizes that an entire agreement is not complete in that it will be influenced and affected by the relation of the parties over time, and therefore requires the flexibility to evolve and adapt the business arrangement to align with the interests and priorities of all stakeholders on an ongoing basis.

✓ **Relationship Management** – Managing stakeholder engagement and communications means expanding communication from one-to-one conversations to a system of coordinated interactions encompassing decisions making, delivery management and oversight processes.

✓ **Collaborative Working** – Having the systems, disciplines, competencies needed to facilitate collaboration and working in teams.

What Is the Relationship Charter?

At the heart of the Relational Model™ operational framework is what we refer to as the Relationship Charter. The Charter which is developed and agreed to jointly by the partners is in effect the platform for Relationship analysis and strategic management, Delivery and performance management and Issues management and resolution. *In the traditional model of contracting, the contract defines and governs the relationship between the parties. In contrast, with the Relational Model™, the relationship as defined in the Charter provides the governing framework for the contract and therefore takes precedence over the contract.* The Relationship Charter advocates structuring a relationship management framework to encompasses three main components:

1. Shared relationship mission and purpose

2. Joint Governance System and Management Processes

3. Open book financial management framework (transparency)

In the following section, we will delve deeper into each of these key elements of the Relational Model™ and describe a basic framework for creating a more efficient structure to manage existing as well as new relationships better.

The Relational Model™: A New Approach That Addresses Outmoded Methods

The Relational Model™ leads to greater cooperation within a contract's framework by encouraging stakeholders to actively seek potential problem areas and reach a mutually beneficial resolution. This approach is contrary to the economic levers referenced by Williamson, which inadvertently support the wrong behavior by punishing disclosure as opposed to rewarding it.

The Relational Model™ promotes a more logical alternative that avoids placing the sole emphasis on missed outcomes. Instead, the objective is to strive toward a state of full disclosure in the delivery process under the umbrella of a Jim Collins' "autopsy without blame approach."

From the standpoint of the vendor selection process, the utilization of the Relational Model™ emphasizes the ability of the parties to effectively and successfully address problem areas as they arise instead of avoiding them.

The Relational Model™ And The ISO 44001 Standard

"The International Standard for Collaborative Business Relationships has now been published by the International Standards Organization (ISO) in Geneva . . . ". - Press Release, March 2017

In the past, measuring or quantifying business relationship success has always been done after-the-fact based on the achievement of the desired outcome.

The challenge with this approach is that it rarely if ever established a definitive and scalable model that could proactively provide guidance. In other words, there was no way to reliably identify the potential gaps in a complex business arrangement and address them, before the initiative was well under way.

Given the continuing high rate of "complex" business relationship failures, something had to be done to create, from the beginning, a consistent approach that maintained the needed balance between a defined process of continual engagement and individual case adaptability.

Consistent with other management standards, such as ISO 9001, ISO 44001 establishes the guidelines for achieving successful relationship outcomes, through the utilization of a "definitive scorecard" that will enable organizations to identify the gaps in their organizations and critical relationships and implement corrective measures throughout the entire relationship period.

ISO 44001 Beginnings

The complexity of doing business demands more than just a mere intent to collaborate. It requires both a commitment and a solid understanding of the changing dynamics in how government and industry do business, and the critical role that relationships play in achieving successful outcomes.

To this end, several collaborative models and corresponding frameworks have emerged over the past decade to address the complexities of public-public and public-private business arrangements. The primary objective of these new models was to move beyond the rigid transactional architecture and mindset that limited collaboration effectiveness by shifting the focus towards the adoption of an adaptive system that drives real change while increasing both individual, as well as common stakeholder value.

The Precursor To The New Standard

Originally established in 2013, the ISO/PC 286 Collaborative business relationship management framework, was proposed by the British Standards Institution in the United Kingdom - otherwise referred to as "BSI-UK." Based on the success of this precursor model in the UK and Europe, the standard migrated to the United States, Australia, and New Zealand as ISO 44001. An international committee was convened to further the introduction of the standard, and currently includes representation from Austria, China, Finland, France, Italy Malaysia, Portugal, Spain, Sweden, and the United Kingdom and the United States.

ISO 44001, presents a real and meaningful opportunity for organizations to both contribute and share best practice methodologies in the areas of collaboration and relationship management.

The Relational Model™: A Practical Approach To Operationalizing The ISO 44001 Standard

The Relationship-based model of Management supports the development and management of an adaptive business relationship among partners, with whom collaboration and ongoing alignment are critical to achieving overarching common objectives. The Framework has been applied with notable success in public-private relationships, as well as in public-public relationships, enabling organizations to deliver improved outcomes consistently. The Relational Model of management operationalizes the ISO 44001 standard which was approved for publication on December 6, 2016, for collaborative business relationships.

As depicted in the diagram below the ISO 44001 standard's focus is on creating and operationalizing two Relationship Management Plans:

Corporate Relationship Management Plan (CRMP) - defines the internal governance system and processes to allow an organization to collaborate effectively with others. At the time of its introduction, effective collaboration was the primary focus of ISO 44001.

The new standard's eight stages of development include:

- ✓ **Awareness** - Establishing the organization's propensity for collaboration

- ✓ **Knowledge** - Evaluating specific collaborative benefits and business case

- ✓ **Internal Assessment** - Assessing the organization's actual capability to collaborate

- ✓ **Partner Selection** - Establishing an appropriate selection process

- ✓ **Working Together** - Establishing a joint governance model for collaboration

- ✓ **Value Creation** - Establishing a joint or common process for continual improvement

- ✓ **Staying Together** – Managing, monitoring and measuring the relationship over time

- ✓ **Exit Strategy** - Establishing a joint or common approach to disengagement

Specific Relationship Management Plan – This a specific plan for a specific relationship with an external or internal party.

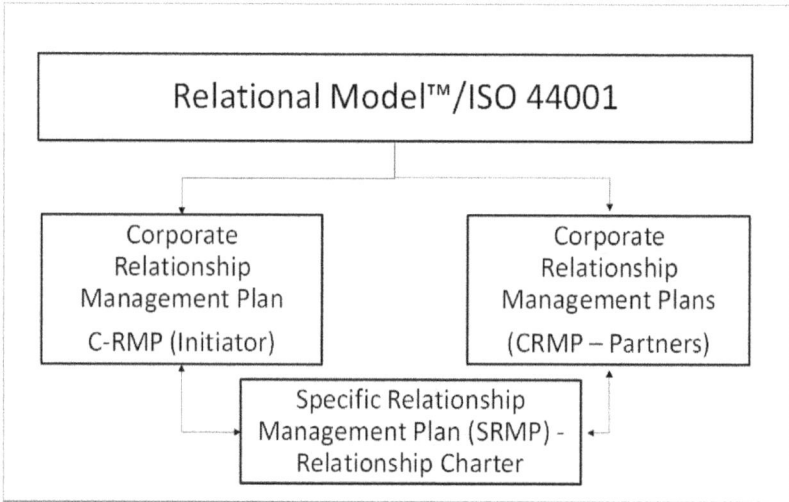

Figure 3: ISO 44001 Architecture

In this book, we make a deliberate attempt to address the SRMP through the relational model and Relationship Charters first. By taking this approach, we will provide a deeper understanding of the foundational requirements for an internal governance and collaborative working system relative to establishing and effectively managing complex collaborative relationships with strategic partners.

Chapter 6

More Insight and Less Oversight!

"The contract must become a platform to manage inevitable change, not pursue certainty based on the original deal." ~ Ian Mack, Director General, Canadian Department of National Defence

As I have stressed throughout this book, the high rate of failure in significant business relationships and large projects is often because public and private sector organizations rely on outsourcing partners who continue to provide their services based on a static requirement at a particular point in time. Relationships structured around these types of models inevitably fail because a single transaction approach does not take into account the natural evolution of needs and stakeholder capabilities.

But what do concepts such as static requirement and "*single transaction approach*" mean?

Quite simply, they mean that when structuring and managing complex relationships, we have to move away from using *similarity heuristic, iterative approximation,* and *equation-based* contracting models.

Past Experience Is Not Always An Accurate Reference Point

Software developers use the *similarity heuristic* to perform debugging tasks. By comparing problem symptoms with those of previously corrected software flaws, a developer can often determine the most probable cause and take remedial action. Over time, a developer's experience allows them to use the similarity heuristic in a highly effective way, quickly choosing a debugging approach that usually reveals the source of a problem.

In the hermetically sealed programming world, using the similarity heuristic makes a good deal of sense especially when dealing with single stream static elements or attributes.

However, in the real world, operational attributes are vastly different. The real world is dynamic and consists of multiple and simultaneous transactional streams. As a result, it does not make sense to take a historical baseline reference approach to problem solving. Doing so results in a myopic view that limits the potential to find solutions.

As I pointed out in my earlier references to the ERP implementation challenges experienced by both TransAlta and Alcan, one of the main reasons why many of the applications of ERP software vendors are ineffective is because of their reliance on equation-based models.

While experience is often a relevant indicator of future performance, the single-stream point of reference associated with an equation-based model can be misleading. This model is especially problematic because it lacks an adaptive capacity through which you can identify, capture and apply real-world variables to produce a sustainable reference model.

Like the similarity heuristic method, these approaches are limited by a "capture once–use many" sequential thought process. For example, the iterative or successive approximation methodology estimates the value of an unknown quantity by repeatedly comparing it to a *sequence* of known quantities.

This approach may seem reasonable, at least on the surface. But similar problems occur when known quantities or declarative values are not dynamically monitored and updated to reflect real-world circumstances, or are too narrow to include all multiple attribute streams that influence a common outcome.

In fact, the reliability of a declarative value of a known quantity diminishes over time as it becomes either too narrow in scope or completely ineffective when the assumptive elements or sequence become outdated. My research has also shown there is an acceleration in the rate of reliability degeneration when there is a lack of understanding relating to known elements due to limited collaboration at the formulation stage.

If we apply these principles to a supply chain practice, it becomes apparent that the iterative model reflects a sequential architecture or thought process that relies predominantly on previously defined attributes in the static chain. These could be purchasing (including indigenous sub-attributes like price, past quality and delivery performance, etc.), tracking and order fulfillment as well as financial reconciliation (internal, multiple streams).

Although the attribute tags themselves remain constant, their assigned weighted value, including those of the corresponding sub-attributes, can and do change at the transactional level. Depending on the weighted importance that is given to each attribute and sub-attribute, combined with the impact of external attribute streams (which are often subject to unanticipated or previously unexpected changes), the cumulative effect will likely and dramatically alter the original model's values.

These shifting values mean that the comparative approximations (including external variables) are static in nature and result in an unreliable comparative model. *Therefore, the traditional application of an iterative methodology that uses a declarative or imperative programming method to define a single attribute stream of practice is largely ineffective in quantifying and managing the supply chain process.*

The failure of many complex relationship initiatives can also be linked to the use of static methodologies that fail to allow for constant evolution. By establishing a single stream, non-adaptive reference baseline, organizations are often forced to institute change-management strategies to align the operational realities of their business with a model that is simply not reflective of how they or their partners function in the real world.

We Need To Build Camcorders, Not Improve Canvases

In a 2005 paper, supply chain expert Jon Hansen[iii] referred to the fact that supply chain software developers need to "build" camcorders rather than improve canvases. At that time, the concepts of agent-based versus equation-based modeling in the general market were not widely understood.

Even though the focus of Hansen's article was on software development, his analogy also applies to the management of complex contract relationships.

Here is the excerpt from that paper. (Note that I have replaced the name of the original vendor with the *ABC Company* moniker.)

Traditional solutions such as those developed by ABC Company are built around what is referred to as an equation-based and therefore focus primarily on the somewhat static interaction between independent entities. (The key words here are static interactions and assumptions.)

Let's consider an example of an artist attempting to paint a portrait of a subject who is in perpetual motion. While the artist may capture for a brief moment a portion of the image on canvas, the reality is that the effort will always be a work in progress. (It is important to note once again, that most e-procurement initiatives take one, two or more years to implement, only to meet customer expectations a mere 25% of the time.)

While you can improve the quality of the paint the artist is using, add more advanced lighting, and even improve brush stroke speed and techniques, the fact remains that the end result is unlikely to change in any significant way. The only way to achieve the desired result is to create an environment where the subject is stationary at all times. To be specific, you have to restrict the subject from moving, from doing what is natural.

Now picture if you will, the same 'moving' subject being captured on film with a camcorder. Regardless of the time of day or changing locations, the subject is always captured in real time. In essence, you are now able to adapt and even interact with the subject's environment. Unlike a painting, when you finish one shot, you can quickly and easily move onto the next, without losing what you have already captured. When required, you have the ability to playback the previous images within seconds.

In this example, you are not asking the subject to change the way he or she operates. Nor are you trying to restrict his or her natural movements. This is at the heart of agent-based modeling. It is also the reason why traditional equation-based applications such as the one offered by ABC Company will never achieve the maximum results in the shortest period of time.

The fact remains that it is imperative to simultaneously engage all parties to a transaction on a real time-basis, with an ability to meet an evolving set of demands as required. Intelligent, strategic sourcing and procurement, through to tracking and fulfillment and finally financial reconciliation with a 'true cost' audit capability is the earmark of a solution which truly leverages the power of the Internet. To effectively develop this type of solution, one needs to abandon equation-based modeling which is driven by the aforementioned interactive assumptions, and replace it with agent-based modeling which is driven by the ability to understand the unique operating attributes of all trading partners on a continuous real-time basis. This leads to a synchronization of independent capabilities, which in turn creates an environment of adaptive responsiveness, producing immediate results in the area of supply chain efficiencies.

We can use Hansen's analogy to understand the complex nature of dynamic relationships better. In many cases, the problem-solving approaches commonly employed by most organizations is akin to an artist attempting to paint a still life subject. No matter how skilled or advanced the artist may be, their tools and techniques will not prove useful in capturing a subject who is in a state of constant motion. In other words, complex relationships by their very nature will not sit still and pose.

The best way to capture the dynamic elements within significant business relationships and large projects requires a different methodology or a "camcorder" such as the Relational Model™. The Relational Model™ ensures that an accurate picture can be captured on an ongoing basis, thereby bridging the chasms between multiple transactional streams.

Multiple Transactional Streams

During the term of a contract, some or all of the following circumstances may occur:

- There is a change in product requirements, service definitions or product/service demands.

- There is a shift in management, e.g., the original executives who entered into the agreement leave.

- There is a change in business requirements.

- Initial vendor "operational" leverage assumptions are weak or the core assumptions relating to an initial deal are proven to be inaccurate.

- Performance Indicators that underpin or drive the pricing models are either not achievable or representative of a mutually beneficial or healthy expected outcome.

- The vendor holds the client hostage to an onerous change order process.

- The expected benefits become harder to harvest than initially expected.

- The contract becomes a vehicle that enables stakeholders to enforce rigid and inflexible terms and conditions that ultimately undermine the relationship.

In the real world, it is very likely that one or more of these changes will co-occur and the challenges they present further compounded. Attempting to corral and manage them under a static contractual framework of an original agreement is sheer folly.

The departure of Steve Durrell from Irving Shipbuilding in November 2012 speaks directly to my point.

Just over one year after winning a $25-billion contract with the Government of Canada, Durrell, company president at the time, left Irving on the eve of a workers' vote to accept a new contract offer.

Some have downplayed Durrell's role in landing the large Royal Canadian Navy deal as well as his influence relative to the pending labor vote. In truth, whenever changes of this magnitude occur in the executive suite of any company, it is anyone's guess as to what the circumstances were that led to the shift or the mid-to long-term impact on the project and its relationships.

Head of Irving Shipbuilding Departs on Eve of Contract Vote
November 27, 2012

Steve Durrell has left his job as president of Irving Shipbuilding, the company confirmed Tuesday evening. (BRIAN MEDEL / Yarmouth Bureau)

Republished with permission from *The Chronicle Herald*

Figure 4: The Departure of Steve Durrell from Irving Shipbuilding

The Three Collaborative Pillars of the Relational Model™ come directly into play with this kind of circumstances.

In the introduction to Section II of this book, I talked about the fact that the contract while obviously, an essential element of any initiative must not take precedence over the Relational Model™ stakeholder relationship. The reason for this position is because it is not possible to achieve a consistent and meaningful alignment of the main success elements without establishing a secure and therefore stable relationship framework.

The ratification of the new ISO 44001 standard gives testimony to the veracity of this position. In fact, this book and the relationship principles it expounds is the defacto implementation "manual" for complex relationships that adhere to ISO 44001.

Relationship Charter

The Relationship Charter defines the relationship and its management model. In general, the Relationship Charter consists of three main constructs:

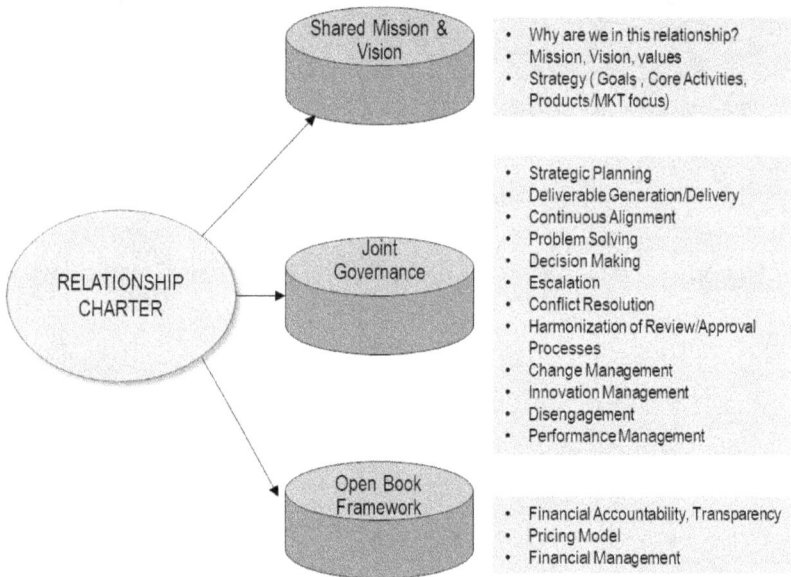

Figure 5: The Relationship Charter

The Relationship Charter is the vehicle through which the "working" relationship framework that is needed to achieve said stability is created and maintained.

Figure 5 above, highlights the Three Pillars of the Relationship Charter Shared Mission and Vision, Joint Governance and Open Book Framework.

I cover these pillars in the next chapter in greater detail along with a framework developed by SRS to monitor all the key success elements of an initiative or program.

Chapter 7

Achieving a Strategic Relational Alignment

"Usually constructed as a moment in time transaction or deal as opposed to being based on an ongoing strategic relationship, traditional long-term business arrangements fail to create, respond to and manage change."
~Excerpt from SRS Relational Contracting Management Seminar

Within traditional contract models, relationship governance adheres to concepts such as Static Key Performance Indicators (KPIs) and associated metrics, service levels, fixed schedules/prices and penalties for missing service level agreement targets.

In such cases, the contract is managing the relationship as opposed to the relationship managing the contract. When unexpected changes occur (as in the case of Steve

Durrell's departure from Irving Shipbuilding), there is an inability to respond to issues such as shifts in executive direction or the unfavorable outcome of a labor vote. While anticipating these as well as other potential circumstances are not usually possible at the time the contract is awarded, they nonetheless present a reality, with which stakeholders must deal.

The challenge is to create a vehicle through which the relationship rather than the contract can respond or adapt to these inevitable changes. In essence, it is important to create a continuous alignment management framework.

Let's begin by defining relational. At the SRS Centre for Relational Contracting and Strategic Management, the definition of relational refers to a process-centric business interaction and delivery management model that promotes collaboration and fosters trust.

In essence, the basis for the provision of a product or service is dependent on a common or joint relationship structure by which contract performance is carried out, measured and evolved.

To reach this point, stakeholders must align with the six criteria outlined on page 51 and restated here:

✓ **Relating** – Connecting and linking in a naturally complementary way.

✓ **Mutuality** – Sharing similar views or outputs.

✓ **Respect** – Recognizing each other's needs, requirements, contributions, abilities, qualities, and achievements.

✓ **Innovation** – Using combined strength and synergies to deliver improved relationship outcomes.

✓ **Empowerment** – Introducing joint management structures and processes for efficient and timely decision-making within scope and envelopes of authority.

✓ **Continuous Alignment** – Making necessary adjustments and business process improvements to optimize outcomes and maximize "achievable" benefits.

A Word About Vendor Selection

Establishing a collaborative, high-performing and dynamic business relationship requires a sourcing process that does not rely on prescriptive procurement mechanisms.

This position relative to vendor selection is particularly important in "future-sourcing" projects, which as discussed earlier, are projects where neither the client nor the vendor has constructed, built or delivered the defined capability, and past work experience cannot solely be relied upon or used as a selection criterion.

In the absence of a proven track record, a closer examination of the vendor's strategy and core capabilities is necessary to determine whether a relationship is likely to succeed.

The Relational Model™ sourcing process includes an intense industry analysis and engagement both before, during and after the actual procurement. This analysis involves the application of advanced analytical tools that objectively assess and evaluate the fit of a vendor's strategy, core capabilities, and resources with the initiative's expected outcome.

When using the Relational Model™, collaboration is born out of common purpose and intent, resulting from a strategic fit. The advanced analytical tools associated with the Relational Model™ are used to determine the veracity of the strategic fit between the client and vendor. This fit is critical in establishing the framework for the Relationship Charter discussed below.

Fundamental Principles Behind The SRS Advanced Analytical Tools

In a procurement framework, competitive analysis and competitive intelligence tools are essential in gaining an understanding of specific industries and organizations within them. These tools can be leveraged to identify the critical points of strategic fit relative to an expected or desired outcome.

Understanding an overall industry rather than focusing on an individual company provides a better comparison of all competitive bidder capabilities, using a single standard that truly aligns with the contracting objectives.

When assessing the goals of the industry as a whole, it is important to ask questions such as: Who are the industry leaders in innovation? What is the industry profitability picture? This assessment garners many critical insights that would not necessarily come to light through a traditional company-to-company competitive comparison.

Consider the retail industry for example.

A Forbes.com article (*Forbes*, 4/24/2007, "Double-digit sales red flag") highlights the link between the percentage of business a buyer represents to a particular vendor and that vendor's level of profitability.[iv] According to the article, although Walmart squeezes the margins of suppliers of all sizes, smaller companies tend to feel a tighter pinch. For example, the beverage company Cott doesn't have the brand strength of Coca-Cola or PepsiCo, whose products are in greater demand at supermarkets, convenience stores, and other outlets.

So Cott, whose primary business is producing and distributing company-brand carbonated soft drinks, turned to Walmart for 38 percent of its sales, compared with less than 10 percent for the two beverage titans. The result? Cott's gross margin of 12.4 percent was about a third of the industry average, while Coke and Pepsi both registered more than 50 percent in the same year.

When considering project partners, it is important to determine the impact overall industry profitability may have in the selection process. By understanding industry profitability from a collective standpoint, you may be able to identify a potential risk that might negatively impact your outcome.

As for the tools themselves, rather than reinventing the wheel, I have used, adapted and leveraged the following tools to achieve the desired results.

Industry Analysis Tools

Although the reason for using advanced analytical tools is evident, there is a difference between acknowledging the value of these tools and using them effectively.

Let's consider the public sector for a moment.

Industry engagement is a critical issue experienced by public sector procurement systems. For many years, governments relied on defining their requirements and then taking them to market in the hope that a vendor (any vendor) would step forward and deliver according to contract specifications.

Unfortunately, this approach abdicates buyer responsibility regarding the successful delivery of the required product or service. For this reason, the government is forced to rely on legal terminology and financial penalties as a means to enforce their desired outcome.

The unintended consequence of this "unilateral" business approach is that it deters supplier participation rather than stimulating active and positive industry engagement.

When Silence Speaks Volumes

A leading industry expert told me that he was surprised to learn during a series of seminars for public and private sector procurement professionals that it was not uncommon for a government tender to receive no responses from the business community. These seminars provided both sides of the tendering process with meaningful insight (perhaps for the first time) and opportunity to understand why responses to RFPs have been steadily declining for many years.

Even armed with this new insight and the recognition that engagement mechanisms have to change, it appears that old habits remain difficult to break.

Although there are signs that there is positive headway regarding a shift in approach, you can still witness the persisting failure to embrace the true spirit of industry engagement through the example of vendor - industry day events in which government makes its upcoming plans known. Even though as many as 100 vendors may attend these sessions, the government does not conduct any industry analysis to determine the critical points of strategic fit relative to achieving expected or desired outcomes. Continuing to rely on traditional acquisition processes through the sending of RFI's, it is business as usual, which includes reliance on secondary sources of intelligence such as Gartner's Magic Quadrant.

Do Your "Own" Research!

In his January 7, 2011, *Procurement Insights* post, Jon Hansen sheds some light on the potential limitations of secondary sources of intelligence:

> *Originally a private company, the Gartner Group was launched publicly in the 1980s, then acquired by Saatchi & Saatchi, a London-based advertising agency, and then acquired in 1990 by some of its executives, with funding from Bain Capital and Dun & Bradstreet. In 2001 the name was simplified to Gartner.*

> *The technology giant, Oracle Corp., was recently named a leader in supply chain planning for its commitment to a streamlined approach to its logistics and supply chain, especially in regard to its technology operations. According to Gartner, the Magic Quadrant assesses vendors within a particular sector based on their 'completeness of vision and ability to execute' supply chain plans.*

> *Despite the accolades, Oracle has had a history of difficult implementations such as with the Veterans Health Administration. In that case, the VHA spent more than $600 million dollars on not one but two failed procurement initiatives. One was with Oracle and the other with J.D. Edwards—a company that was ironically purchased by Oracle in 2005.*

Case examples like these raise an important question; upon what was Gartner's assessment of Oracles offering based?

This apparent disconnect has drawn into question the validity of Gartner, Aberdeen and other analyst firm findings, resulting in the general market's 'growing cynicism' In their ability to provide comprehensive industry intelligence.

Hansen then goes on to cite several reasons as to why analyst firms seem to fall short in their analysis. For example, he questions the depth of their expertise and objectivity relative to their assessment of a rapidly changing global marketplace.

Whether or not you agree with Hansen's assessment of the secondary intelligence market, one thing is clear: conducting your "own" analysis is the best route to take. In other words, leveraging industry analysis tools guarantees that your insights will be void of any interests other than your own as well as those with whom you chose to do business.

Porter's Five Forces

Porter's *Five Forces Analysis*[vi] is a framework used for industry analysis and business strategy development. Created by Michael E. Porter of Harvard Business School in 1979, it draws upon industrial organization economics to derive five forces that determine "competitive intensity" and resulting "market attractiveness."

Attractiveness in this context refers to overall industry profitability. An unattractive industry is one in which the combination of these five forces drives down profitability. A very unattractive industry would be one approaching pure competition, in which available profits for all firms are driven to "normal" profit. For the sake of clarity, normal profit is the "minimum level of profit needed for a company to remain competitive in the market."

1. **Threat of new competition**
   Markets that yield high-profit returns will attract new firms. The increase in the number of new entrants will eventually decrease profitability for all firms in the industry. Unless incumbents can block new firm entry into the market, the abnormal profit rate will tend towards zero (perfect competition).

2. **Threat of substitute products or services**
   The existence of goods outside of the realm of established product boundaries increases the possibility that customers will switch to alternatives produced by competitors. For example, tap water might be considered a substitute for Coke, whereas Pepsi is a similar product produced by a competitor. Increased marketing for drinking tap water might shrink the pie for both Coke and Pepsi, whereas

increased Pepsi advertising would likely grow the pie (increase consumption of all soft drinks) and give Pepsi a larger slice at Coke's expense.

3. **Bargaining power of customers (buyers)**
Bargaining power of customers involves the market of outputs and the ability of customers to put the firm under pressure, which can also affect customer sensitivity to price changes.

4. **Bargaining power of suppliers**
Bargaining power of suppliers involves the market of inputs. Suppliers of raw materials, components, labor and services (such as expertise) to the firm can be a source of power over the firm, especially when there are few substitutes. Suppliers may refuse to work with the firm, or charge excessively high prices for unique resources.

5. **Intensity of competitive rivalry**
For most industries, the intensity of competitive rivalry is a major determinant of competitiveness. Competitiveness may be dependent on:

- Sustainable competitive advantage through innovation

- Competition between online and offline companies

- Level of advertising expense

- Powerful competitive strategy

- Flexibility through customization, volume, and variety

Porter's Five Forces And The Relationship Charter From A Buyer's Perspective

The Walmart example cited earlier in this chapter provides a good example of how Porter's Five Forces come into play.

The ability to offer customers a cheaper private label brand alternative (e.g. Cott) as well as premium brands such as Pepsi and Coca-Cola, provides Walmart with a competitive advantage over other retailers. In this way, it can offer a product range that satisfies a much larger consumer base than if it sold either only a low-cost product or a premium beverage brand.

The potential risk is that Cott is forced to operate at a much lower profit level than the industry average. Even if the company wasn't in danger of going under, there still might be a potential impact on product quality. In any event, the buyer (Walmart) would have to turn to alternative suppliers for its private label line.

The Cott case demonstrates the importance and value of assessing a partner's viability on an ongoing basis, especially within the framework of the Relationship Charter discussed earlier.

Even though Walmart can exert tremendous leverage upon Cott to drive down costs, they must still weigh the risk of having to find a new private label partner against increased profitability. This paradox is an important point of consideration, especially if the popularity of the private label brand proves to be exceedingly high.

On the other hand, if Walmart was to place too much pressure, it may force Cott into bankruptcy in much the same way it did with Vlasic Pickles (a Walmart supplier who succumbed to the company's price point strategy).

If Cott went bankrupt, Walmart would need to find a new private label manufacturing partner or pursue an alternative strategy similar to Delta Air Lines. Delta was forced to buy an oil refinery as part of their fuel category management strategy. According to the Humphrey and Schmitz (2002)[vii] Value Chain Governance Model, the latter option would require that Walmart makes the transition from its present quasi-hierarchy relationship with Cott to a hierarchy governance model, in which they would assume a direct ownership position.

By using the Relationship Charter, the lines of meaningful communication would remain open so that both parties could work collaboratively towards achieving a mutually beneficial outcome. Leveraging the Charter in such a manner could eliminate or at least reduce the risk of an unexpected challenge.

Even with an open line of transparent communication between stakeholders, it is essential for Walmart to assess the industry as a whole.

The Fourth Pillar

The ability to assess the ongoing viability of existing relationships represents the Fourth Pillar of the Relationship Charter.

While the three core pillars of the Relationship Charter Agreement focus on the active management of the relationship between stakeholders, the Fourth Pillar does not directly involve the delivery partner or partners. It is used to establish a contextual industry reference point outside of the existing relationship(s). It also provides ongoing checks and balances that ensure the continuing viability of a strategic fit between existing stakeholders. In this way, the Fourth Pillar maintains the integrity of the entire initiative by assessing its relational veracity and capabilities through a comparative analysis of external broader industry developments.

Relationship Charter

The Relationship Charter defines the relationship and its management model. In general, the Relationship Charter consists of three main constructs:

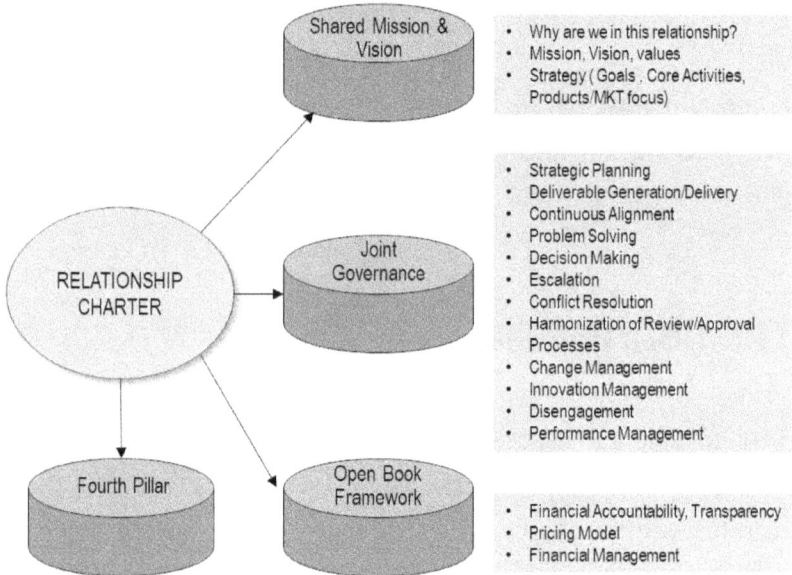

Figure 6: The Relationship Charter – Fourth Pillar

Adaptable "Readiness"

The question of alternative strategic relationships invariably arises when considering the continued viability of existing relationships and the critical role of the Fourth Pillar in maintaining integrity.

If the sustainability of a current relationship is in question, what is the best course of action?

When a potential stakeholder viability issue arises, the initial or first step is to look to the existing relationship or relationships for a possible remedy. Only when it becomes clear that the stakeholders cannot address the identified problem area(s) should the pursuit of alternative solutions outside of the Relationship Charter framework be considered.

For example, as reported by the Military Analyst Ken Hansen on December 20th 2012, the proposed militarization of the Canadian Coast Guard could have meant that the work originally earmarked for Irving might have gone to another supplier outside of the present bi-directional relationships network because Irving, supposedly would not have time to retool their current manufacturing facilities to meet the changed requirements. However, in this case, it is unlikely that the government would look outside of the existing network to bring in a new vendor because the Navy's contract also included a second supplier, Seaspan Shipyard.

Because Seaspan can build ships that meet the proposed new "militarized" requirements, they can address the significant directional strategy shift on a timely basis. This adaptable readiness demonstrates the value of strategic grouping.

In essence, the practical use of the industry analysis tools at the beginning of the acquisition process can ensure that ideal partners are identified for originally intended tasks as well as for their ability to adapt to changing scenarios within the existing relationship framework.

As illustrated by the Canadian Coast Guard example accomplishing an internalized transfer of stakeholder capabilities within a current relationships network is achieved through the application of different strategies such as splintering.

A Word About Splintering

In their January 2011 *McKinsey Quarterly* article *Building the supply chain of the future*, Malik, Niemeyer, and Ruwadi[viii] wrote:

> *Getting there means ditching today's monolithic model in favor of splintered supply chains that dismantle complexity and using manufacturing networks to hedge uncertainty.*

There is a fair amount of misunderstanding surrounding the concept of splintering. In my relational contracting seminars, I often hear the comment; "but you can't always splinter your procurement." Statements such as these are attributable to the belief there would be an unproductive overlap of capabilities if two companies were capable of building, for example, the same ship. This is true, but each company can definitely build half the number of ships or build certain components of the ship with less overlap and more specialization. This will also support the creation of sustainable sector as I discuss later in Chapter 8.

In such a scenario, the creativity and experience of the sourcing team come into play, as do the Relationship Charter and the Fourth Pillar.

In short, creativity, experience, and adaptability ensure that stakeholders, and in particular governments, avoid becoming hostage to an inflexible business arrangement through utilizing what I refer to as a "load balancing" approach. I will discuss this last point in more detail in the next section on strategic grouping.

Strategic Grouping

A "strategic" group[ix] is a cluster of companies within an industry that have similar business models or strategy combinations. For example, you can divide the restaurant industry into strategic groups such as fast food and fine dining based on variables such as preparation time, pricing and presentation.

The number of groups within an industry and their composition depends on the dimensions used to define them. A two-dimensional grid is often used to position firms along an industry's most significant plane.

Understanding an industry's "dimensional plane" helps distinguish direct rivals (those with similar strategies or business models) from indirect rivals. The ability to better understand the strategic direction and respective business models of direct rivals within a group provide a transitional capacity similar to what occurred or could have occurred with Irving and Seaspan. This ability to efficiently and reliably "load balance" reduces risk by increasing the collective group's adaptability to both known and unknown business variables.

A Strategic Group Analysis will identify rival organizations with similar strategies and business models for inclusion within a strategic group referencing the following characteristics:

- Extent of product (or service) diversity
- Extent of geographic coverage
- Number of market segments served
- Distribution channels used
- Extent of branding
- Marketing effort
- Degree of vertical integration
- Product (or service) quality
- Pricing policy

Strategic Group Analysis is also useful in a variety of other ways.

Besides identifying direct competitors and on what basis they compete, Strategic Group Analysis also indicates if there is a possibility that one organization might move from one strategic group to another, and the resulting opportunities and strategic problems this could present to both existing as well as new contracts.

Strategic Group Analysis And The Entrepreneurial State

One point of a digression at this particular juncture is worth noting; I believe that it is incumbent upon the government to assume a proactive role in using its buying power to drive innovation and build industry sectors. Strategic Group Analysis that seeks to identify the strategic direction and business model viability is the perfect tool for accomplishing these objectives.

However, to get to what Mariana Mazzucato referred to as being an entrepreneurial state, Canada must move away from the Build in Canada Innovation Program (BCIP) "supply push" approach, and adopt the U.S. Government's Small Business Innovation Research (SBIR) "demand pull" model.

With the former, startups (and tech innovators) are asked to present technology that's almost ready for the market, at which point BCIP "shops" it to government departments.

The "demand pull" model of SBIR sees U.S. government entities identify problems they are trying to solve and then challenges startups to come up with innovative solutions. In other words, they are driving innovation and therefore stimulating industry development and growth.

Sourcing Relationships And Strategic Grouping

In chapter six and chapter seven respectively, we discussed the contract award to Irving Shipbuilding and the advantages of multiple transaction streams using the example of changes to the Royal Canadian Navy contract and the need to engage Seaspan.

Unexpected changes like these are not limited to contract specifications alone.

Steve Durrell's departure from Irving on the eve of the vendor's pending labor negotiation brings to mind a similar situation that occurred with the appointment of a new chief legal counsel at a critical juncture in my efforts to save the TransAlta account.

As was the case with me and the introduction of a new chief legal counsel, I would imagine that there was a good deal of uncertainty and with it questions when Durrell announced that he was leaving Irving.

What if Irving's new president had reservations regarding the pricing model used by his predecessor to win the Navy business? After all, $25 billion represents a large opportunity *and* a large risk. (Just ask EDS about their experience with the Navy Marine Corp contract, and that was only a $7 billion deal).

Concerns about Irving were fueled further when, just before the former president's departure, the company announced that it was seeking to overturn Ottawa's decision to release portions of the umbrella agreements relating to the contract.

Signed earlier that year as part of the national shipbuilding procurement project, Irving expressed concerns over the sensitive nature of the documents and requested that they remain private.[x]

Although Irving eventually decided not to pursue this action and accepted the public disclosure of the terms of their agreement with the Royal Canadian Navy, it was nonetheless a disquieting turn of events.

According to Military Analyst team leader for the Maritime Security Policy Program at Dalhousie

University, Ken Hansen, the idea of redirecting significant segment of the contract to Seaspan would add unsettling impact on the relationship dynamic. Especially since the building of the Arctic patrol boats could be taken away from Irving entirely.[xi]

The reasons behind this possible change provide an excellent example of the concept *of multiple transaction stream influence* **AND** the importance of managing relationships effectively.

According to media reports citing secret memos, when learning of the Canadian plans, the United States government pressured the Canadian government to militarize the Canadian Coast Guard as a way of beefing up the defense forces in the region. This "change" in specifications meant that large, heavily armed icebreakers would replace the small boats. Although Irving was expecting to build this type of larger frigates, it had not anticipated that work would start until the second stage of the contract a couple of years down the road, which would have given Irving enough time to tool up for the frigate work.

A Canadian government decision to militarize the Canadian Coast Guard vessels could mean that the contract would have to be redirected to another supplier because Irving did not have the necessary time to shift directions to accommodate the new strategy. Alternatively, and for economic reasons, the government could also choose to provide Irving with the timeline and support for the retooling process.

But are these the only options?

As mentioned earlier, in addition to Irving, the Royal Canadian Navy contract included a second supplier, Seaspan Shipyard in Vancouver. Given that Seaspan could build these larger ships means that a "known" stakeholder who is already a party to the same network could step up to meet the requirements associated with this proposed significant directional strategy shift.

In the situation such as the one above using the Relational Model™ strategic group mapping exercise as part of the original procurement process would have paid tremendous dividends.

The reason is quite simple.

At the time the contracts were awarded to Irving and Seaspan, the alleged diplomatic pressure from a foreign government was not part of the equation. However, if Relational Model™ strategic group mapping had been incorporated into the selection process early on, the resulting Relationship Charter would have been written in a manner that could have removed the uncertainty of change for all stakeholders, including of course Irving and Seaspan.

Even if Seaspan did not have the capacity to fulfill the new contract requirements, using the Relational Model™ strategic group mapping exercise would have put the government in a proactive position. The reason; the government would have already identified potential

> **Author's Notes**
>
> *One of the biggest shortfalls of the umbrella agreement is the absence of a relationship management and collaboration framework.*

alternative suppliers through the Competitive Analysis and Competitive Intelligence procurement framework.

Without an effective relationship management framework, unexpected change can force all parties into a reactive position, in which decisions made both now and, in the future, will likely have unintended consequences on the economy and foreign policy as well as other strategic national objectives.

The Diamond-E Framework

The Diamond-E Framework, developed by Michael Porter, can be used to analyze the structural, cultural and process-oriented elements of an organization, and to determine how these factors relate to a company's business strategy.

Dividing the framework into two sub-groups; an internal group (consisting of management preferences, organization, and resources) and an external component (environment), their level of alignment with company strategy can be analyzed both individually as well as jointly. This exercise helps to identify deficiencies or gaps within each sub-group, providing insights into how they relate to each other and the strategy itself. If gaps or deficiencies emerge, the company can correct the component-specific issues or make the appropriate changes to their strategy.

While adopting Porter's Five Forces and the Strategic Grouping tools for the Relational Model™ made sense, I decided to reshape the Diamond-E Framework into a predictive model. This "overhaul" was possible with the Diamond-E as it was originally developed with an evolutionary capability so as to maintain its relevance through the introduction of newer versions. In fact, since first being introduced by Joseph N. Fry and Peter J. Killing in 1986, xii there have been a total of six updates to the Framework.

In modifying the Diamond-E Framework, I have converted it into a Relationship Fit Triangle specifically suited for strategic procurements.

As depicted in the graphic above, I have extended the core Diamond-E elements beyond an assessment of the veracity of an organization's strategy to include a consideration of their impact on Benefits Realization Factors (BRF™). SRS established BRF™ in 2003 as a

STRATEGIC FIT ASSESSMENT
STRATEGY-OUTCOME PREDICTIVE EVALUATION

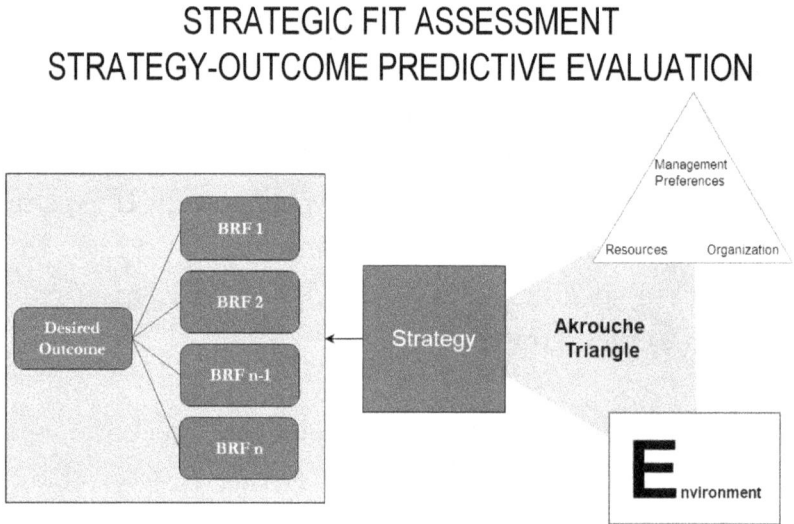

Figure 7: The Relationship Fit Triangle

means of defining the variables or key factors that must be enabled to achieve success relative to the expected outcome.

Similar to the Critical Success Factor (CSF) concept originally developed by D. Ronald Daniel of McKinsey & Company in 1961 (and later refined by John F. Rockartx[iii]), was conceived as a means to illustrate *outcome realization factors*[xiv] that the procurement world encounters on a regular basis.

An extended focus on specific industries (or functions within specific industries as depicted by the Akrouche Triangle) is not uncommon. For example, in 1995, James A. Johnson and Michael Friesen[xv] extended the CSF concept to many sector settings, including health care.

However, the relationship of a BRF™ to a procurement initiative outcome is more like the relationship of a CSF to project management and risk factor in risk management. It is a necessary element needed to harvest the benefits associated with an acquisition. It is likely that most procurement professionals can recall at least one initiative where, despite the success of one or two critical factors the expected outcome of an overall initiative was never realized.

BRF™ And The Health Care Industry

There are multiple industry sector examples where the failure of critical success factors within a joint initiative proved to be catastrophic.

The VHA's inability to successfully implement both an Oracle and JD Edwards' purchasing platform spanned a period of seven years and cost American taxpayers $650 million. This failure was costly from a financial standpoint, and ultimately its ramifications on patient care led to a series of Congressional hearings.

During a March 2004 hearing, then Secretary for Management William H. Campbell acknowledged that "there are considerable concerns over the implementation of an automated system and its potential effects on medical care at one of the VHA's largest facilities, Bay Pines Medical Center in Florida."

According to an Office of Inspector General's report, problems such as a failure to convert inventory data within the system resulted in the cancellation of procedures including life-saving surgery due to a lack of critical medical supplies.

Many factors led to the failure of the VHA initiative leading to a gain of needed insight into the automation of health industry procurement practices. For example:

- Decisions should be made based on a vendor's industry-specific expertise and ability to deliver a viable solution.

- Communication and collaboration mechanisms within a health care facility are essential to ensure maximum levels of compliance.

- Clearly-defined and well-established performance response mechanisms that identify problems quickly and efficiently are needed to avoid an adverse impact on the quality of patient care.

The final point above illustrates why any approach to the automation of the healthcare industry's procurement practice must include a BRF™ centered on patient care delivery.

Individual BRF™ can serve as critical success touch points that can impact the overall success of any initiative provided they are part of the Relationship Charter's Shared Mission & Vision Pillar.

In this regard, the Akrouche Triangle provides the starting point for connecting or bridging the assessment of a vendor's strategy with the BRF™ elements that are critical to achieving the desired result.

The first step is to measure the tension or link between a Bidder's Strategy components and BRF™.

The second step is to determine how well the strategy is supported by core internal and external elements, including:

- **Resources** – Does the company possess the required resources to execute the strategy? Do they have the right mix of assets and underlying capabilities to enable and sustain the strategy? (internal factor)

- **Organization** – Does the bidder have the core organizational capabilities that will enable and sustain the strategy in the long term? (internal factor)

- **Management Preferences** – What is the bidder's management preferences and experience and how does it fit with current or communicated strategy? (internal factor)

- **Environment** – What is the competitive position of the firm and how will competition influence its strategy and ability to execute on the strategy? (external factor)

This straightforward and efficient two-step process transforms the Diamond-E Framework into a predictive model that can be used to test the degree of fit and alignment between vendor strategy and capability with BRFs and to identify the negative factors that undermined not only the VHA procurement initiative but all similar undertakings.

As stressed previously, the start of the acquisition process is the ideal application point for the Akrouche Triangle. However, there are often many projects struggling to achieve expected results, and this tool can be utilized at any point in time to put an initiative back on track by aligning a vendor's strategy with the buying organization's BRF™.

McKinsey 7S Framework

The McKinsey 7S Framework[xvi] is a management model developed by well-known business consultants Robert H. Waterman, Jr. and Tom Peters in the 1980s. The 7S's include structure, strategy, systems, skills, style, staff, and shared values.

Based on the theory that these seven elements must be aligned and mutually reinforcing for an organization to perform well, this model is often used to assess and monitor internal changes within an organization. The model can be used to help identify needs that require a realignment to improve performance or maintaining alignment (and performance) during other types of changes.

The model also helps us understand how organizational elements relate to each other during changes such as restructuring, the introduction of new processes, corporate mergers, new systems, changes in leadership, etc.

The purpose of the model is to analyze how well an organization is positioned to achieve its intended objective and can, therefore, be used to:

- Improve the performance of a company

- Examine the likely effects of future changes

- Align departments and processes during a merger or acquisition

- Determine how best to implement a proposed strategy

Both the Diamond-E Framework and the McKinsey 7S Framework share similar characteristics. As previously stated, decomposing and then rebuilding the Diamond-E as opposed to the McKinsey 7S into the Relationship Fit riangle (RFT) was made easier because of its inherent pliability.

Like the Diamond-E Framework, the 7S is an excellent tool for continuously assessing and measuring the alignment of relationships within an intended objective. Unfortunately, neither model has proven its usefulness from a procurement standpoint.

The Akrouche Relationship Fit Triangle was designed specifically for the procurement world. Selected attributes of the McKinsey 7S Framework were rearranged to complement further the key characteristics of the Diamond-E to address the challenges associated with a complex acquisition process.

Value Chain Analysis

The concept of supply or value chain implies a sequential architecture that is no longer applicable in a world where most organizations' supply practices involve the synchronization of diverse stakeholders that may span multiple supply networks.

The value chain concept was first introduced by Michael Porter in 1985 in his book, Competitive Advantage: Creating and Sustaining Superior Performance.[xvii] According to Porter, as products pass through each point in the value chain (referred to as activities), they gain added value. This singular stream progression is why the structure or architecture of the chain is sequential rather than synchronized.

For example, a diamond cutter's costs in cutting a diamond may be minimal, but the service he provides in cutting the diamond increases its "collective" value when it becomes a finished product. As Porter stresses, it is important to differentiate the value from the actual cost of the related activity.

The assignment of added value takes on greater importance in the emerging global marketplace, especially in critical areas such as the development of viable supply clusters both domestically as well as internationally.

The Public Sector Value Chain

Throughout this book, I have provided reference points to both private as well as public sector enterprises, mostly on a separate or distinct basis.

The value chain concept illustrates the discernible bridge between the two sectors. This difference is of particular importance because complex government procurement activity must take into account factors such as the impact on the economy as a whole, foreign policy as well as other strategic national objectives.

In short, government procurement is not just about building a ship or buying fighter jets.

In their book *Clusters Facing Competition: The Importance of External Linkages* (2005), Giuliani, Rabellotti and van Dijk[xviii] describe the value chain perspective as extending beyond the realm of manufacturing to include "other activities in the supply of goods and services, including distribution and marketing" (Kaplinsky, 2000; Wood, 2001).[xix] This broad definition allows for the possibility that the government might initially assume the role of lead firm and leverage the competencies of domestic clusters (or supply chains) to satisfy its internal requirements.

The expansion of the procurement function might be

used as a springboard to develop competencies that ultimately establish the viability of domestic stakeholders (ex., small and medium-sized enterprises, or SMEs) on the global stage.

Author's Notes

For more on the latter, refer to van Dijk and Wang's analysis in Chapter 10 regarding the Chinese government's role in "speeding up the growth process of a software cluster firm in Nanjing," including the link with that country's national innovation system (e.g., universities and associations.)

In order to leverage domestic competencies, we must fully understand and assess the capabilities of the "heterogeneous" supply community in servicing public sector needs. This exercise also helps identify areas of global strength or leadership within a particular industry.

Unfortunately, the public sector often fails to look beyond the promise of limited savings through spending reduction. As a result, most purchasing initiatives advocate a vendor compression strategy where direct contracts with larger entities are expected to drive volume savings.

Unfortunately, these savings rarely materialize as hoped. The most significant and negative consequence of a compression strategy is its impact on the development and sustainable growth of a cluster. According to Goldstein,[xx] a cluster is "a spatial concentration of firms (including specialized suppliers of equipment and services and customers) and associated non-market institutions (universities, research institutes, training institutions, standard-setting bodies, local trade associations, regulatory agencies, technology transfer agencies, business associations, relevant government agencies and departments, etc.) that combine to create (or deliver, per Kaplinsky and Wood) new products and/or services in specific lines of business."

If we accept Goldstein's definition, any factor that hinders the stakeholders' ability to collaborate (such as a myopic focus on spend reduction) naturally creates a tense atmosphere that limits cluster development both domestically and globally.

It is interesting to note that those opposed to globalization share the same concerns as the detractors of supply-base rationalization. According to Heakal,[xxi] opponents of globalization fear that the effects of expanded business-seeking economies of scale will negatively impact small businesses (who are the primary stakeholders in a cluster). As a result, "competition could virtually disappear as large companies begin to integrate and the monopolies created focus on making (or from a buyer perspective, saving) a buck."

An October 2002 U.S. report entitled *A Strategy for Increasing Federal Contracting Opportunities for Small Business* issued by the Executive Office of the President raised serious concerns about the negative impact of public sector contract bundling on the SME community. This report also suggested there was retardation within the innovation process, which many believe is a fundamental tenet of an active SME (cluster) base.

This last point regarding the innovation process takes on greater importance when you consider that most innovative breakthroughs happen at the SME level and that from these advancements, additional, perhaps more significant, savings can become a reality. As a result, government's need to take the lead in fostering SME innovation, as emphasized earlier when I talked about Mazzucato's "Entrepreneurial State."

Beyond savings, a sound strategy for identifying, developing and engaging industry specific clusters (of which SMEs are an integral component) domestically, can also help governments to position these same organizational bodies to compete and succeed on a global basis. Because of this, it is incumbent upon government organizations to evaluate all areas of spending from a combined strategic vantage point, and where possible, leverage (or develop) cluster core competencies.

According to Humphrey and Schmitz (2002), "value chain research focuses on the nature of the relationships between the various actors involved in the chain and on their implications for development." These authors emphasize that governance is an essential element of a value chain and coordination is required "to make decisions not only on 'what' should be, or 'how' something should be produced but sometimes also 'when', and 'how much' and even at 'what price.'" (Note: the same questions that apply to production also apply to purchasing decisions.)

Although coordination may occur through arm's-length market relations or non-market relationships, the latter applies best to government procurement practices. Within non-market relationships, Humphrey and Schmitz identified the following three possible types of governance;

1. Network, implying cooperation between firms of more or less equal power which share their competencies within the chain;

2. Quasi-hierarchy, involving relationships between legally independent firms in which one is subordinate to the other, with a leader in the chain defining the rules to which the rest of the actors have to comply; and

3. hierarchy when a firm is "owned by an external firm." [xxii]

The network mechanism makes the most sense from a national public sector procurement standpoint only if the more traditional government hierarchy mindset can reconcile itself with an implied equality of power.

Author's Notes

The Three Pillars of the Relationship Charter can be indispensable as a mechanism for managing a complex relationship.

For example, a network governance structure has succeeded in the Chinese software industry. According to Van Dijk and Wang, "software companies express what they expect from the government and local government." Eager to promote the sector, the government was "very willing to act upon their suggestions." [xxiii] This high level of collaborative interaction is demonstrated when local authorities push relations with universities and local research and development institutes. This collaborative approach represents a pattern of governance that is commensurate with a network-type structure.

If Canada and the United States are to compete in the emerging global economy, they must take note of the attitudes and actions of China as well as other world players (e.g., the European Association of Development Research and Training Institutes). By doing so, they are likely to conclude that the development and utilization of indigenous or domestic clusters in which SMEs are most prevalent should be a key building block for global economic success.

According to a study referenced in the book, Clusters Facing Competition: The Importance of External Linkages, by focusing on the interaction between internal clusters and external linkages, governments will be able to determine how these interactions will help SMEs to face increasing global competition. One of the best ways to gain this understanding is through direct participation as a buying stakeholder.

The Relational Model™ Synergy Framework

Synergy takes place when two (or more) elements work together to produce a result greater than the sum of their individual effects.

The Relational Model™ represents a synergistic amalgam of the best attributes of each of the tools discussed above. The adoption or adaptation of these "tools" focuses on making sure that the model will enable clients to achieve

126

their objectives, regardless of the diversity of their requirements.

Achieving the above-referenced synergy was the result of extracting and where necessary, modifying the viable elements of a variety of existing analytical tools into a collective whole that can identify and address the relationship needs of all stakeholders. Because initiatives will be successful only when the needs of all parties are aligned and met, this approach has proven to be effective time and again.

In the final pages of this section, we examine the executable aspects of the Relational Model™, including a detailed outline of the SRS dynamic Joint Governance, Accountability, and Performance Management Framework (GAPM®). GAPM® was developed by SRS as a baseline model for implementing relationship management frameworks in the public and private sectors.

We will then close out the section with a summary of the differences between a traditional and Relational Model.™

As an added benefit, I will also revisit and review in the Appendix in greater detail the Three Pillars that make up the Relationship Charter, using highlights from actual case studies.

Continuous Alignment Management Framework

Once you have established a relational fit with a vendor or vendors, you can make the transition from a traditional governance model to a continuous alignment management framework. Making this change can be accomplished through GAPM®.

As illustrated below, the structure of GAPM® reflects an ongoing relational cycle. It applies a dramatically different approach than the sequentially static and myopic traditional governance model, in which the emphasis was on achieving an "end" result (e.g., product or service delivery).

The latter approach is inherently flawed because it is reactive. Evaluation of the major success elements such as stakeholder capacity and best practices does not take place until after there is a product or service delivery problem.

If you refer to the section on vendor selection (page 44), you might be inclined to suggest that avoiding such problems through the use of a proper due diligence mechanism during the supplier qualification process, is the answer. However, and as emphasized throughout this book, the real world is not static, and circumstances change. Relying solely on conditions from a historical point in time as the basis for future performance is

tantamount to dressing for yesterday's weather report—
it is a failure waiting to happen.

Fundamental issue: Long-term "business arrangement" is constructed as a
"moment in time transaction" or a "deal," and not as an ongoing strategic
relationship able to create and manage change.

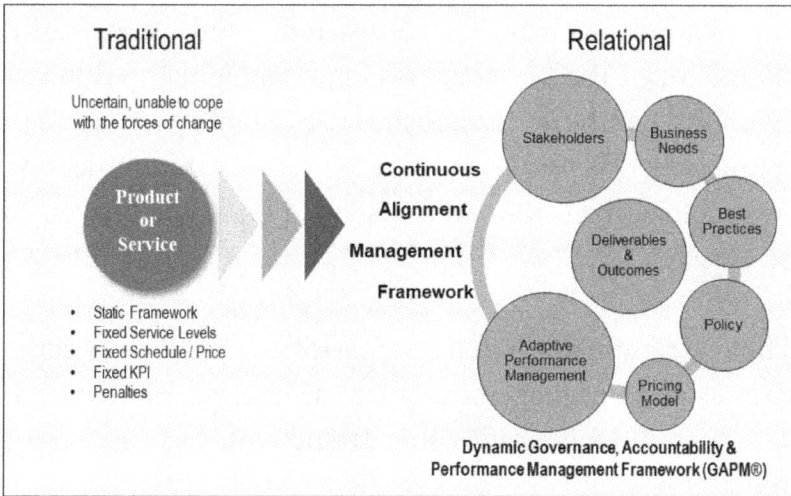

Figure 8: GAPM® Structure (1)

GAPM® is proactive and provides an opportunity to
address issues before they become problems, through a
continuous alignment of the major success elements with
the delivery expectations of a product or service.

Achieving this state of ongoing alignment requires that
the relationship between all stakeholders be evaluated
and understood on a continuous basis. The Relationship
Charter plays a primary role in this evaluation process.

Revisiting The Three Pillars Of The Relationship Charter

As I had stressed in the introduction to Section II, when using the Relational Model™, stakeholder relationships need to take precedence over a contract. In other words, you cannot achieve a consistent and meaningful alignment of the key success elements highlighted in the GAPM® without establishing a stable relationship framework. Without a stable relationship, meeting contractual objectives on a sustained basis has proven to be elusive.

The Relationship Charter (ISO 44001 Specific Relationship Management Plan) is the vehicle through which a working relationship framework can be created and maintained.

Figure 4 on page 67 depicts the *Three Pillars of the Relationship Charter: Shared Mission & Vision, Joint Governance, and Open Book Framework.*

Shared Mission And Vision

In the world of strategic planning, organizational mission and vision provide context, direction, and guidance to employees who are working together to achieve a particular enterprise outcome.

Mission and vision are also important in relationships. The First Pillar of the Relationship Charter focuses on how stakeholders derive context, direction, and guidance from the mission, vision, and values of the relationship.

This virtual collaborative organization operates under a shared vision through which both the collective and individual interests of all stakeholders are understood and satisfied.

Mission and vision are the ties that bind stakeholders together and help them establish a common set of values. Throughout this book, I have referred to the failed EDS-United States Navy contract where focus shifted from service delivery to financial recovery. In this case, the fallout for both parties was significant financially and operationally.

> *Had both EDS and the Navy established a clear "shared" mission and vision strategy, the challenges that ultimately undermined the initiative would have been preventable.*

When I say preventable, it is with the understanding that many of the factors that contributed to the failure of this project would have likely been detected beforehand using the industry analysis, and engagement mechanisms discussed earlier in this chapter. The fact that the problems went undetected underlines the importance of objectively assessing and evaluating the fit between the vendor's strategy, core capabilities, and the initiative's expected outcome.

Even after the application of these tools and the awarding of the contract, the continuing evolution of trust between partners is critical for sustained success. For this reason, the ongoing alignment process should not cease with a contract award.

The How Is As Important As The Why

How we form a mission and purpose for the relationship is exceedingly important. In other words, it should not be a paper exercise offering platitudes of intent in place of a meaningful game plan. Producing positive results such as in the case of TransAlta requires the establishment of an iterative consultation and convergence process that ties the mission to the realization of relationship objectives both individually as well as collectively.

If this level of collaborative communication had taken place, it might have produced a much more positive outcome for VHA. It certainly would have allowed all stakeholders to come together to synchronize individual needs and objectives into a shared strategy that would have resulted in a vastly improved outcome for all concerned.

With the above in mind, a collaborative communication process should include the following steps:

1. Define your expected outcome and associated benefits.

2. Define your benefits realization factors (BRF™).

3. Initiate dialogue to gain a shared understanding of the whole purpose of the relationship.

4. Develop a draft mission and vision using an iterative convergence process to review and refine the mission, purpose, and values.

As referenced in the case study in Appendix A, which illustrates how a partner-oriented dialogue with the selected vendor (now partner) might occur, this is where the Relationship Charter comes into play.

Joint Governance (Working Teams)

A team is a small number of people with complementary skills who are committed to a common purpose, performance goals and approach for which they hold themselves mutually accountable (John Katzenbach & Smith, 1993).

You cannot begin to structure a joint governance framework until you have established a mutual mission and vision that leads to an ongoing, shared (as opposed to transactional) relationship.

By applying the principles of the Relational Model™, team members shift their perspective. They cease to view each other as members of differing organizations and begin to connect by sharing the experience of pursuing a mutually beneficial goal. As in any relationship, however, getting to that level is hard work.

Most business relationships begin with a shared desire among all parties to work together to achieve an outcome that is important to each one individually. It is at this point that the questions that can test the relationship arise. These include:

- How do we work as a team?

- How do we align our activities to achieve the overall objectives of the relationship?
- How do we structure ourselves to manage the generation of deliverables?

- How do we learn together, decide together and continuously improve together?

- How do we write flexible contracts?

- How do we benefit from institutional learning and risk management?

- How do we balance the priorities of individual stakeholders with the priorities of the group?

- How do we entice stakeholders or their agents to focus on our mutual objectives?

- How do we support our teams as they transition through the forming, storming, norming and performing stages?

- How do we train new team members as people transition in and out of the relationship?

- How do we make the necessary adjustments to achieve our objectives on a continuing basis?

Even if we were to address all of these questions fully, the sustained success of the "joint" governance framework for the relationship is directly proportional to the actual degree to which the joint teams function as a single or cohesive unit.

For many, this last point raises a red flag, as it is already challenging enough to attain focus and cohesiveness when all stakeholders belong to the same organization.

Achieving the required focus and cohesion can become even more of a daunting task when the stakeholders come from different organizations.

These are of course legitimate concerns. However, if developed properly, the outcomes of a joint team endeavor can be far greater than the individual interests of any one stakeholder. In other words, the collective needs of the many ultimately outweigh the needs of the one, especially when there is a defined mission and vision that point the way to a successful outcome.

My reasons for such a positive outlook are as follows:

1. A shared mission and vision in which there is a precise definition of both collective and individual outcomes provide a solid foundation upon which to build a working relationship.

2. The understanding that leveraging the collective strength and complementary resources of the group creates opportunities that would not have otherwise been available.

3. There is pride in achievement.

Within the context of the above, here is what the joint governance framework would look like from a structural standpoint:

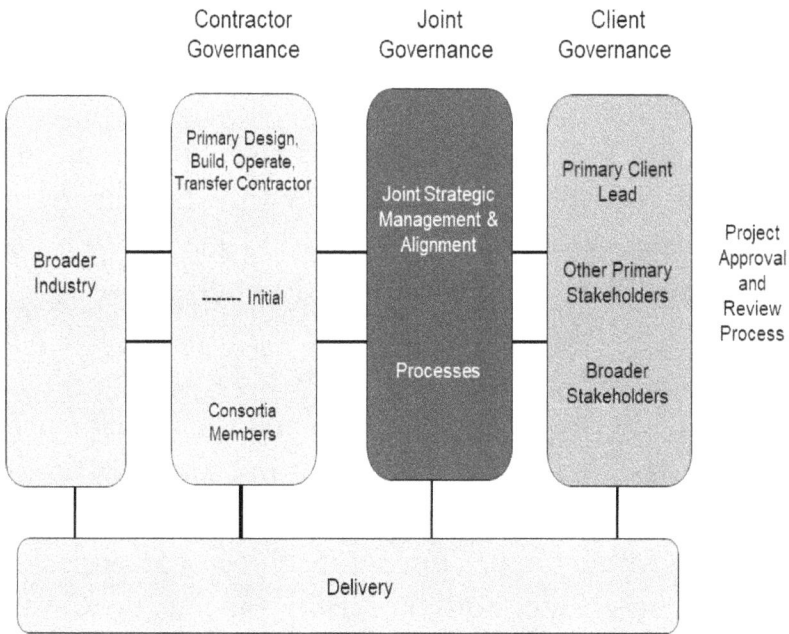

Figure 9: Relationship Governance

Typically, a joint governance framework incorporates three different classes of governance structures that are interrelated and need to work together to support the objectives of the relationship.

Usually, the client and contractor have their indigenous governance structure, and so the joint governance component of the framework serves as a bridge to incorporate the individual interests of each stakeholder into a unifying execution mechanism.

The joint or common governance component is the means of bringing together the shared mission and vision elements of each stakeholder in a manner that ensures ongoing alignment with the project's best interests.

Only after an open discussion takes place in an atmosphere of mutual trust regarding the best interests of the shared project can the underlying interests of both the client and the contractor be understood and served.

It is important to remember that although the joint governance component of the extended governance relationship is a driving force, it is not an island unto itself. The ability to continually facilitate two-way dialogues with both the contractor and client governance components ensures both the vitality and integrity of the joint governance efforts.

In this context, there are three governance structures in a relationship:

- A joint governance that makes up the union of the stakeholders.

- A "right governance" that represents the mechanisms and processes of the buyer side.

- A "left governance" that addresses the processes and the workings of the provider side and the entire supply chain.

Because initiatives are inherently horizontal, it is critical that the joint governance teams have broad visibility across the whole relationship spectrum.

Unfortunately, having this level of visibility is usually easier said than done, especially within the public sector.

In fact, one of the most critical challenges I have experienced is governance misalignment resulting from limited visibility.

Within the public sector, alignment is extremely challenging because of the existence of legislative silos. Silos can hinder collaboration in potential areas of shared stakeholder interests. The existence of these silos leads to the creation of independent initiative streams in which the duplication of effort and cost will become the norm.

The following example illustrates a typical result of a dysfunctional right governance model:
The same vendor might be used by multiple departments to provide similar solutions, which could be better delivered at a much lower cost if horizontal integration were available. Because of the lack of broad spectrum visibility, it is not uncommon for one government department to pay considerably more than another for the same product or service from the same vendor.

When this collaborative dysfunctional model includes external relationships, there is an imbalance of benefit in favor of one partner over another. This imbalance is often the reason why so many initiatives fail.

The Open Book Framework

When one partner's financial viability is compromised either unintentionally or through a lack of consideration, there is a relational imbalance. Righting this imbalance can be problematic as achieving an honest, trust-based collaborative relationship requires the existence of financial transparency in the relationship.

There is no doubt that an adversarial or protectionist mindset is the quickest way to derail any initiative as it reflects a lack of transparency. Take Irving Shipbuilding's request to keep the terms of the umbrella agreements as part of the national shipbuilding procurement project secret. Even though Irving stated that the basis for the privacy request was because the documents "contained sensitive information that should not be made public" the actions prompted taxpayers to suspect that they may be hiding something. Under such circumstances, even if seemingly justified, a lack of total transparency makes it difficult for partners to work collectively towards a common goal, particularly if the information necessary to succeed is not provided to all stakeholders.

The open book framework provides the critical information and financial performance (or nonperformance) visibility that will ensure a fair and equitable gain is identified and maintained for all stakeholders. Achieving mutual gain through pricing metrics that reflect a full cost or "target" full cost, and includes a transparent incentivized pricing model, provides the catalyst for all parties to work together to achieve the desired outcome.

In the procurement field, this usually means improving the business process across the entire value chain. The result leads to better quality and financial performance that in turn, is shared by all parties in the relationship. This shared economic outcome provides the vendor(s) with an additional competitive advantage and an incentive to participate in an open book framework relationship.

On page 5, I gave you an overview of the impact that EDS's mounting losses with the Navy contract had on their relationship, and ultimately the fulfillment of the contract. As I pointed out, trying to make something work on the fly based on the transformational model benefits no one. With EDS facing continuing losses and market pressure, they shifted their focus from service delivery to one of financial recovery. This inward-looking strategy, which is hardly the foundation upon which to build a long-term, win-win relationship, represents a fatal disconnect within the Third Pillar of The Relationship Charter. It is, in fact, the ultimate deal breaker regardless of whether the contractor walks away or stays in the game.

Unfortunately, and as is the case with the majority of tendered business transactions the level of "openness" that would lead to the disclosure of financial challenges is not only absent from relationships, it is usually discouraged. In fact, an admission on the part of the contractor that they are experiencing financial difficulties can trigger any number of unwanted reactions including the possibility of termination!

Transparency And The Relationship Charter

The Relationship Charter establishes the building blocks needed for a trusting relationship. By focusing on continuous alignment, there is an ongoing evolution of trust, without which disclosures of any kind, especially those involving financial viability, would be impossible.
I had often wondered what might have happened if, before EDS's financial woes became public, the former IT giant had established a relationship or governance structure that allowed a more open, two-way communication between the company and the Navy. The resulting transparency might have prevented many of the client controversies that led to the ultimate failure of the contract.

The £709 million claim of the British TV company, BSkyB against EDS over the latter's "failure" to meet, agreed service standards is also worth noting at this point, especially given the former's assertion that these failures resulted from fraud stemming from the original contract discussions. If true, this illustrates a "let's win the business first and worry about making it work later" mindset on the part of EDS. The problem this creates is that the vendor is only considering top line numbers without a real understanding of the actual cost of delivering to contract specifications.

However, and to be entirely fair, BSkyB's method of selecting a contracting partner was (at least in part) a contributing factor to the eventual failed outcome. In a blind leading the blind scenario, but if BSKyB had utilized the Relational Model's™ advanced analytical tools to objectively assess and evaluate the extent of the strategic fit between themselves and EDS, the events might have played out very differently.

Even with the selection of EDS as the winning contractor, use of the GAPM® along with the creation of a Relationship Charter would have quite likely identified and possibly prevented problems long before litigation became the only course of action.

At this point, it is important to note that the effectiveness of the Relational Model™ is not limited to new business relationships but can also reinvent and strengthen the performance of existing relationships as well.

The Difference Between A Traditional And A Relational Model™

There is, needless to say, a stark difference between traditional models of engagement and The Relational Model™.

The traditional models are what I call remedial-based, focused on risk mitigation resulting from an initial set of assumptions that may or may not reflect an accurate picture.

Conversely, The Relational Model™ represents an enablement-based framework. While the former focuses on managing the relationship to avoid failure, the latter focuses on how to achieve success. While one reflects a transactional relationship between stakeholders, the other seeks to source a "relationship" with properly aligned partners.

I made this statement during an interview with procurement expert Jon Hansen in response to a question regarding the main difference between a traditional, complex contracting model and the Relational Model™.

The above conversation took place well before the news broke that the Government of Canada was mulling over the viability of a new procurement agency for the expressed purposes of procuring "ships, planes, trucks, and all the other extraordinarily expensive and frequently controversial gear required by a modern military."

In the context of the above news, let's revisit the contract award to Irving Shipbuilding as a typical example of a traditional engagement. Now I have openly used this example throughout this book to explain the Relational Model™ within the context of a current real-world challenge. However, the Canadian government's dealings with Irving are by no means unique to Canada, as all public entities to varying degrees follow a similar track.

Recognizing the Relational Model™ applicability to any government contracting process, I will draw parallels with the Canadian government's contemplation of two possible options for managing massive acquisition projects.

For some time now, the Canadian government is considering the possibility of;

1. rolling out individual secretariats for each successive military procurement (as was done in the fall of 2011 for the Royal Canadian Navy's new fleet of warships), or

2. consolidating an estimated 10,000 bureaucrats from three federal departments (Defence, Public Works, and Industry Canada) into a single massive new agency, under the aegis of a single minister.

In my opinion, either option might work, as the government's thinking indicates that they are in the right room relative to finding a solution. However, their proposed structures highlight the fact that they have not yet turned on the light.

The biggest problem with the proposed options is that neither goes far enough in establishing a framework for managing the post-acquisition relationship. In essence, it is akin to providing someone with a new car, but not putting any gas in it. It may look good and promise a good ride, but it won't get you out of the parking lot.

Or to put it another way, awarding the business is not the same as realizing (or managing) the desired outcome. So, how do you manage to achieve the desired outcome? Unfortunately, both options disconnect the procurement of a long-term business relationship from the operational or fulfillment considerations that are essential for sustainable success. These considerations include factors such as the overall impact on the economy, foreign policy and other strategic national objectives. Specifically, it is not just about building a ship or buying fighter jets. It is about meeting the seemingly disparate yet undeniably interconnected   interests of different stakeholders simultaneously and consistently.

In their efforts to address these relational challenges, the government is correct in acknowledging that there is a problem. However, success will likely remain elusive until the framework for managing the relationships between these various stakeholders becomes part of the process either at the beginning of an acquisition or some later point by a willing group of stakeholders.

The point is this; until there is a viable relationship model in place, any proposed changes to the procurement process itself will not produce the desired outcomes.

I am not alone in my thinking, as Jon Tattrie shared a similar opinion in his Atlantic Business Magazine article "Ships Will Start Here (Eventually)." Tattrie deftly points to the fact that managing expectations were the biggest challenge for Irving in the wake of the $25-billion contract win. Unfortunately, managing stakeholder expectations have to transcend the individual project-oriented silos that are commensurate with the current government project-based approval and oversight process.

In this regard, I would recommend the establishment of individual secretariats as opposed to a consolidated, centralized organization under the following guidelines:

- Each secretariat includes all stakeholder representatives to ensure that collective interests are understood and appropriately managed on an ongoing basis.

- There be a defined focus on specific types of procurement.

- There would be built-in flexibility to adapt to potential changes in factors such as market conditions or stakeholder capabilities as a means of ensuring the best outcome.

- Finally (and similar to the United States VHA's structure) each secretariat would be held accountable for their expected outcome.

To be able to hold them accountable, the secretariat's must first receive the right tools to manage the complex stakeholder relationships associated with significant acquisitions.

While each of the above guidelines is important, the ability to adapt to unforeseen changes is particularly crucial. If you source long-term relationships with a project mentality, it is tough to identify or even respond to the inevitable changes that may occur over the life of a contract. The reason for this is fairly obvious—historic experience is no guarantee for future success. Nor can you adequately address future or unanticipated contract/relationship risks through the typical financial inducements, or increased oversight of a project-centric approach that ends with the procurement itself.

Based on all of the reasons cited above, we have to start sourcing relationships as opposed to transactions or deals. At the end of the day, "sourcing" relationships represent the new paradigm in contract management, and it is the defining difference between the traditional and relational models.

Section III

So What Is The Deal Anyway?

In the first section of this book, I talked about the timeline for transformation in complex contracting, while in the second section I provided a practical understanding of what this new paradigm means.

In this third and final part of the book, I will focus on the concept of the deal within the deal being the need to source and manage relationships within a traditional performance-based contracting model.

In complex, long term arrangements, performance-based contracting is inherently adversarial. It creates an unbridgeable chasm between stakeholders and adversely impacts collaboration and a shared, mutually beneficial outcome.

The performance-based model has, at least in the past, been the de facto framework in contracting, especially in military acquisitions. It is my opinion (based on guarded optimism combined with a practical realization) that this model on its own, is outmoded and change is inevitable. Having said this, I do believe that that the inclusion of a relationship management framework will enable performance-based contracting to work.

In several recent Department of National Defence workshops, the SRS team has facilitated the development of a relational management framework between internal and external stakeholders that has elevated buyer-supplier collaboration resulting in a "progressive" transition to productive outcomes.

How Relational Frameworks Make Performance-Based Contracting Work?

Performance-based contracting (PBC) is about "buying performance, not transactional goods and services."[xxiv]

At the beginning of a sourcing process, the performance-based contracting model may appear to provide the ideal manageable framework for achieving the critical milestones related to a desired outcome.

As shown in the following diagram, this model relies on an analysis of known factors to gain the necessary insight into creating the path to actual objective realization in which the vendor compensation is in alignment with achieving the prescribed milestones.

But what happens if insights into the known factors represent only a partial picture?

What if there are changes that may either positively or negatively affect the chosen path towards the intended objective?

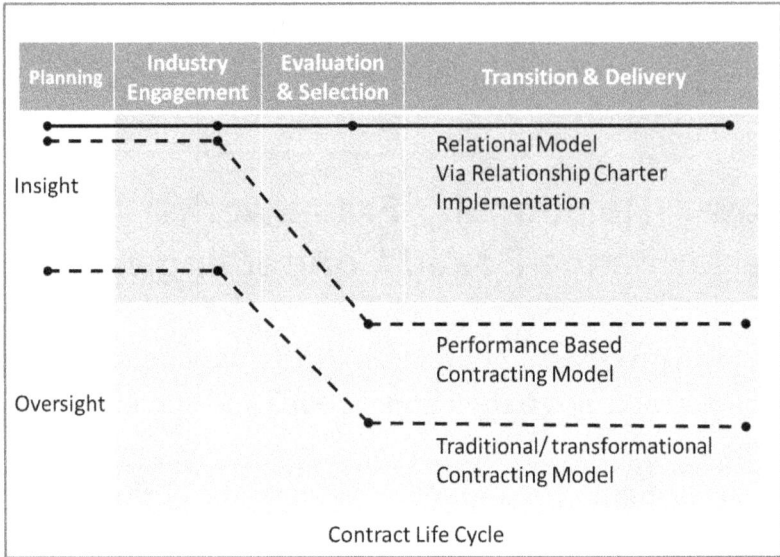

Planning	Industry Engagement	Evaluation & Selection	Transition & Delivery

Insight

Relational Model
Via Relationship Charter
Implementation

Oversight

Performance Based
Contracting Model

Traditional/ transformational
Contracting Model

Contract Life Cycle

Figure 10: The Performance-based Contracting Process

Unfortunately, once the contract is signed in the performance-based contracting model, stakeholders are focused on managing the deal as opposed to the relationship. Overlooking the importance of the relationship to maintain contractual terms and conditions means that there is little incentive to expand stakeholder understanding beyond the prescribed or pre-determined path.

In fact, rather than rewarding outside the box (or in this case path) thinking, financial incentives force all stakeholders to make the performance-based track work even if it amounts to placing a square peg into a round hole.

This "forced fit" provides yet another example of how the performance-based model manages through oversight and compliance while the Relational Model™ manages through collaboration and insight.

Why would anyone opt for being a participant in a performance-based only initiative?

The answer is fairly standard, for many who have experienced the fallout from a bad client-vendor relationship, it is possible that a performance-based contract provides them with a false sense of security.

The term performance-based implies that payment is made only for value delivered. While equating payment with the "value" received may sound like a good way to ensure a desired outcome with minimal or no risk, some situations can and do arise that fall outside of everyone's control. For example, what if the product or service no longer provides the same value, especially if a better alternative becomes available down the road? What if there is a change in requirements or dealing with a future sourcing arrangement where neither party has experience? The I-35 bridge contract in Minnesota immediately comes to mind with this latter point. When these common situations occur, where does that leave your program or strategic initiative?

In reality, it is the "value received" static parameters that form the foundation of the performance-based model that underpins and undermines the performance of the business arrangement throughout the lifetime of the relationship.

To address the problem, you must get beyond the "sourcing deals as opposed to relationships" mindset reflected in the narrow and restrictive elements of a performance-based model.

In the final chapters of this book, I provide a roadmap for navigating the evolution (or perhaps revolution) in making the transition from transactional deal-making to collaborative relationship building in the complex contracting process.

We will begin by identifying the obstacles to change, and progress through why change is necessary and what practical steps must be taken to establish this exciting new paradigm.

Chapter 8

When It Comes to Change, Gleicher Knew What He Was Talking About

The key according to Gleicher is to isolate the actual problem areas of change and develop unique strategies specifically designed to resolve the correct form of resistance. ~ Excerpt from the white paper Utilizing an Intelligent Filtering Platform to Enhance Contract Performance[xxv]

Created by Richard Beckhard and David Gleicher Gleicher's Formula for Change is a model that "illustrates that the combination of organizational dissatisfaction, vision for the future and the possibility of immediate, tactical action must be stronger than the resistance within the organization for meaningful changes to occur.[xxvi]

In explaining the core elements of resistance to change, Gleicher states that "resistance to change is often referred to as the cost of change. It is then subdivided into the economic cost of change (monetary cost) and the psychological cost of change. What this tries to demonstrate is that even if the monetary cost of change is low, the change will still not occur should the psychological resistance of employees be at a high level and vice versa."

Or to put it more simply, the prevailing "we have always done it this way" mindset often trumps the potential financial gains associated with doing something different. While the private sector is not immune to such thinking, it is within the public sector that a change in the approach to "complex" acquisitions faces the greater resistance. The CF-18 Hornet initiative (discussed later in this chapter) immediately comes to mind.

I do not want to oversimplify the reasons why organizations, especially within the public sector, continue to utilize the traditional adversarial performance-based model in spite of the resulting losses of taxpayer dollars. However, and in the following article from August 2007, xxvii Jon Hansen highlights the issues in his review of a paper comparing the differences between public versus private sector commodity buying tendencies.

Government Procurement: A Misinterpretation Of Failure?

Hard evidence is needed to provide an accurate gauge of DoD spending efficiency. This study which examines DoD spending on specific items shows that DoD spends significantly less than their private sector counterparts on similar items. These findings question the widely-held beliefs about the inherent inferiority and inefficiency of DoD purchasing practices. The findings also argue for much more careful research on purchasing and acquisition, so that the likely effects of reforms are known.

Major Joseph Besselman (USAF), Ashish Arora, and Patrick Larkey Purchasing Performance: A Public Versus Private Sector Comparison of Commodity Buying (1999)[xxviii]

To adequately assess the 2006 DoD Implementation of Strategic Sourcing Initiatives Report, I reviewed several Defense Department studies spanning a period of several years. This exercise included the above referenced 1999 report that analyzed the differences between private and public-sector commodity buying practices. The reason for this approach is that it created a much broader understanding of how the DoD procurement process has (or hasn't) evolved over the past ten year period.

This window of review is considered to be important even to those who are not employed within the public sector, as many pundits now believe that DoD procurement practice represents the ideal model for overall "best value" efficiency.

This "time lapsed" look provided a unique insight into defense spending, and the then current attitudes and circumstances that ultimately helped to define DoD policy today.

Based on the figures the government had available at the time of the report, the DoD had spent $132 billion dollars on goods and services in 1996. These expenditures encompassed 8.7 million contracts. Ten years later (2006), the DoD's total spend on goods and services was more than $265 billion dollars.

Initial Obstacles To Understanding And Change

As a result of the general perception of DoD procurement inefficiencies and the resulting waste of taxpayer dollars, the 1999 report's authors encountered several road blocks in their efforts to gather pertinent data reliably.

These included:

- *The "myriad abstruse rules and procedures" government buyers had to follow to purchase items.*

- *The difficulty in comparing items of like makeup. The report cited video tape recorders as an example, indicating that the units utilized in military jet aircraft were different from those purchased by the regular consumer.*

- *The media's "exploitation of past anecdotes of alleged incompetent buying" (i.e. the $436 hammer) fueled the general atmosphere of fear amongst DoD sector personnel. Throughout the report, the study's authors made reference to the concerns surrounding the expectation that their findings would portray DoD staff in an unfavorable light. What was interesting is the authors' indication that "leadership within the DoD itself" was perpetuating this fear.*

- *The reluctance on the part of some commercial entities (suppliers) to participate based on the belief that the data associated with their sales activities was of a proprietary nature.*

As a means of addressing the above concerns and thus ensuring access to critical data, the identity of report participants remained secret. This commitment to confidentiality the authors believed was essential, as it alleviated the fear on the part stakeholders that their practices and outcomes would prove embarrassing or in the case of suppliers undermine their competitive position.

Beyond reluctance, on the part of interested parties the ever increasing level of public cynicism regarding institutional creditability and performance, which was made worse by highly publicized incidences such as the 1998 spare parts scandal mentioned in the report, only served to hinder productive action. These factors, the authors claim had unnecessarily shifted the focus away from what they referred to as the big picture, which they determined was the large dollar expenditures.

I am inclined to agree that a continuing climate of mistrust impedes open and honest communication (the "autopsies without blame" principle referenced in Jim Collins' book Good to Great comes to mind). However, solely focusing on big picture purchases undermines the authors' overall neutrality. This limited view was an important (and fortunately the only) misstep in a paper that delivered valid findings, as it could to the casual reader suggest an attempt to justify poor performance in other areas. Areas which unfortunately tended to grab the biggest and most sensational headlines.

Study Synopsis

The 1999 report attempted to answer the question "is there systematic evidence to support public beliefs" concerning the efficiency (or inefficiency) of purchasing practices within the DoD. As indicated earlier, this is a question that can reasonably be extended to include both public and private sector organizations.

I believe that the "true" importance of this exercise was not to either condone or condemn DoD buying performance, but to provide the impetus to question, develop and implement where required superior procurement practices. And I believe that it is this very mindset that has indirectly led to the 2006 Strategic Sourcing Initiative.

While it is important to recognize the fact that this book's focus is on complex acquisitions as opposed to commodity buying practices, what stood out for me as I read this article and the corresponding paper is that obstacles to change are similar regardless of the type of purchase, or the financial outcome!

For example, the authors of the report encountered several roadblocks in their efforts to gather pertinent data. These included a fear of exposure on the part of DoD personnel relating to potential process failures, supplier resistance to share information, and the restrictive nature of "onerous" procurement policies. So even though the DoD commodity buying department was doing their job, it was only after some persuasion and the promise of anonymity that the report's authors could get to the truth.

In the private sector, the *2013 Procurement & Strategic Sourcing Data Survey*[xxix] has revealed that the majority of CPOs believed their company's short-term goals undermine long-term value. Specifically, 65 percent of

CPOs focus on using competitive pressure to get maximum value from suppliers, rather than using collaboration to achieve the same results (35 percent).

"Chief procurement officers are challenged with the task of driving savings and delivering critical resources with maximum value," said Paul Mandell, founder, and CEO of Consero. "Our survey reveals a conflict for chief procurement officers, who want to obtain the best overall value, yet often rely on competitive pressure rather than collaboration. Procurement officers should communicate to senior management that pursuing unreasonable short-term savings can be destructive to long-term value" Mandell concluded.

Once again, we are discussing commodity purchasing as opposed to a single complex contract, which on its own can cost taxpayers billions of dollars. If there is resistance to openly communicate (which I believe is a prerequisite for change to take place) with relatively straightforward commodity purchases, then one can only imagine how much more challenging open collaboration will become with a single, large-dollar complex acquisition.

And this is my point! With so much on the line in complex contracting, taking the same rigid transactional approach associated with commodity buying virtually guarantees failure. The reason is quite simple; by reducing essential stakeholder relationships to mere transactional engagements, you limit your ability to communicate effectively on an ongoing basis.

However, the move away from static performance-based contracting and the associated change order mentality is a big risk for some. Prior to the Relational Business Model and ISO 44001, we were, to some degree, asking buyers and their departments to let down their guard and expose themselves to the risk of failure, without providing them with the proper model to succeed.

Referring to Gleicher's formula, the only way to overcome this contradictory stalemate between existing process and desired outcome is to "isolate the actual problem areas of change and develop unique strategies specifically designed to resolve the correct form of resistance."

In other words, we cannot simply entice people to take the risk to try something new without providing them with the means or strategies through which said changes guarantee positive results.

Therefore, the best way to facilitate change is to eliminate risk, which means that it is necessary to both understand and establish a relationship management framework.

An Example Of What Not To Do: CF-18 Hornet Replacement Strategy

A common thread of thinking continues to persist regarding the ability of governments globally to affect the kind of positive strategic changes we have discussed earlier in this chapter.

Let's consider the controversy surrounding the Canadian government's proposal to replace the aging CF-18 Hornet fighter jets with F-35 Joint Strike Fighter planes.

The contract for the F-35 JSF planes is telling. The media reported the contract was canceled after estimated costs soared from $9 billion to $45 billion. This jump was staggering and should have sounded alarm bells about the effectiveness of the original acquisition process. However, rather than change their approach, the Canadian government engaged a reputable consulting firm to develop a second plan, a plan which turned out to be virtually the same as the original process leading to the F-35 result.

My expressed opinion about the second proposal and the Life Cycle Costing (LCC) framework in a 2015 post is as follows:

It provides nothing that one couldn't find in a managerial or financial accounting academic textbook. I am not surprised the Treasury Board (TBS) adopted this approach because it supports the current TBS framework for approval of complex capital projects, which by the way, I have been trying to change with some success.

In any case, the issue is the same; the second proposal is trying to bring price predictability into the selection of a long-term relationship, which we know does not work. Although the proposal recognized the need to be innovative (which is good), it was focused on the wrong metrics and used the wrong tools. Life Cycle Costing or LCC (which, as we explain in our seminar and our online training program, is an ongoing cost analysis option) cannot be used to predict cost, based on primarily an initial set of inputs and assumptions. I don't even think it would be legitimate to select vendors on this basis. So, net-net, I doubt that the outcome in this procurement will be any different than previous acquisitions of the same kind.

As it stands now, the Royal Canadian Air Force remains stuck with the aging CF-18s. Meanwhile, the time consuming "Doom Loop"—a term used by Jim Collins in his book *Good To Great* to describe an initiative or program that consistently fails to gain traction—contracting process using the LCC framework, grinds slowly towards yet another failure.

So, what is the answer?

In the next chapter, I assume a Monday morning quarterback position and provide my game day strategy for a successful complex contracting acquisition, using the CF-18 case as a reference point.

Chapter 9

Focus on Building Relationships that Create Sustainable Value

I am not pro or against the technology, I just want to build value in Canada. So let's take the focus off of politics and technological leanings and place it where it best serves everyone's interests. What I am talking about is leveraging the proper industry analysis, applying strategic vendor capability assessment tools and building the relationships that are necessary to create sustainable value in Canada. If you do that you will inevitably make the right decision.[xxxi]

The above statement was my response to a question from the media in January 2013 regarding the controversy surrounding the F-35 situation and a paper released by the Conference of Defence Associations (CDA) Institute.[xxxii]

Before I describe in detail the specifics of my proposed strategies, some context is necessary regarding how the F-35 story ties into the CF-18 replacement acquisition.

The authors of the F-35 paper and the CDA Institute appear to be indirectly championing the fighter jet as the right answer for Canada's military needs. This approach seems to represent a preordained choice and is likely to eliminate other options that could be more suited to achieving the desired outcome when it would make more sense to base a decision on a proper industry analysis that takes into account the diverse interests and goals of all stakeholders.

In other words, the paper appears to stack the deck in favor of the F-35 by suggesting the utilization of a new procurement framework to explicitly select the fighter under the proposed "international model for defense procurement scheme." Is the F-35 the right choice? Experience has consistently demonstrated that averting the usual procurement regime in favor of a preferred or expedient option discounts the best interests of all stakeholders.

In my opinion, following the course of action suggested by the paper would ultimately lead to abandoning a focus on investment in Canada. It is hardly the ideal scenario under which Canada should develop its capability to build weapon systems of significant military value. Especially since it would also mean that a select few American, United Kingdom, French and German corporations would become the de facto primary suppliers. Canada's national role would then be little more than that of a great consumer of and tier 2 supplier of defense systems and support services. In practical terms, this course of action would all but eliminate the possibility of using procurement to promote innovation, commercialization, and jobs in this country.

So, what would be the ideal scenario? A mutual engagement in which there are no winners and losers, but opportunities for mutual gain.

For example, by focusing on the maintenance of the fighters, Canadian firms could become proficient in a particular niche strategic area of the value chain as well as a tier 2 or 3 supply capacity.

In this regard, let's examine more closely Canada's Industrial Technology Benefits/Value Proposition or ITB/VP.

Economic Imperatives

To start, and as alluded to multiple times in this book, government's must both recognize and embrace the reality of what Mariana Mazzucato called the "entrepreneurial state."

For Canada to move in this direction, the government has to take the lead in much the same way that China took the initiative with its robust software industry.

In his article Public Sector Procurement Practice and the Principles of External Economies, Clustering, and the Global Value Chain, Jon Hansen wrote the following about China's active role in helping its software industry to "participate and compete in the emerging global economy."

"An example of where this governance structure has succeeded is in the previously referenced China software industry where according to van Dijk and Wang, "software companies express what they expect from the government and local government, eager to promote the sector, is very willing to act upon their suggestions." An example of this high level of collaborative interaction is when local authorities "push relations with universities and local research and development institutes." According to the authors, this represents a "pattern of governance" that is commensurate with a "network type" structure."

When Hansen talked about a "network type" structure, he was referring to the level of cooperation between stakeholders and how they share their competencies within the chain to everyone's mutual benefit.

With the above in mind, the primary goal of the ITB/VP policy is to ensure that "Canadian industry benefits from government defense and security procurement."[xxxiii]

In short, the ITB/VP is a crucial instrument for SME innovation, which (as everyone would agree) is the engine of our economy. The question we have to ask ourselves is if we are doing enough to enable Canadian business to compete on a global stage. At least this is one of the questions that I would ask.

With the old Industrial and Regional Benefits program - which was the precursor to the ITB/VP, there were those who contended that actively working towards achieving the IRB policy goals would result in higher costs to build warships and weapon systems. While this may have been the case with IRB, the same voices of opposition have not expressed similar concerns with the ITB/VP - yet. Even if it were the case, an investment in the country's industrial base would create an economic endowment in Canada meaning that its benefits would far outweigh any additional initial costs for generations to come. I am not just talking about creating more jobs here. What I am referring to is progressing and securing the country's economic position in the world by developing the all-important tertiary and quaternary industrial sectors.

The quaternary sector is considered to be an extension of the "three-sector hypothesis of industry." Established by Colin Clark and Jean Fourastie, the "sectors" includes the extraction of raw materials (primary), manufacturing (secondary) and services (tertiary). The quaternary sector, which is the engine that drives both innovation and expansion, consists of industries that provide information services such as computing, information and communication technologies, consultancy, research, and development.[xxxiv]

Because this transitional hypothesis process took place over many years, the groundwork for our current system spans different eras and political regimes. About my earlier reference to using government procurement to achieve industrial presence and strength in the global economy, we again need to ask the following question: Has the government done enough to stimulate development and growth (including re-training) through each sector for future generations?

Given the significant cuts in recent years to Department of Defence budgets, the fact that we would potentially reduce our industrial stake in remaining contracts such as the F-18 Hornet replacement undertaking to that of a spectator, suggests that the answer to this question is no.

It is important to note that this is a bipartisan issue that should not solely rest at the feet of the current government. Adherence to the "true" intent of the IRB policy is critical because it will transcend political agendas and affiliations.

One of the key elements of a successful CF-18 replacement acquisition initiative is the fact that the procurement should drive immediate economic benefit and the progression of our economy within an increasingly globalized marketplace.

In this instance, the key stakeholders are the Canadian public. Their representatives at the table should be politically appointed individuals such as a minister or a deputy minister.

Another question comes to my mind is this: why doesn't Canada have a national aerospace strategy to drive and support our efforts and the Canadian firms in the sector?

Military Needs

Whether or not (at least from an economic standpoint) the F-35 is the best choice, we should not overlook the fact that the needs of the military are of paramount importance vis-à-vis stakeholder interests.

In this regard, the following reader response to a recent article I wrote on the F-35 is worth noting:

> *I don't know if it is good or bad for the economy, but the day the CF18s can't fly anymore is the day we'd better have something else ready to throw up there. At that point, the economy becomes secondary to our survival as a nation. All this talk of sustainable value, TCO, etc. becomes of secondary importance when someone flies [something] into our airspace and all we have left are Cessnas and a couple of Bombardier executive jets. Imagine our economy the day after...would it be good or bad then?*

Even though I appreciate the reader's position, I disagree that it is an either-or scenario. What happens if we abdicate our military technological intelligence to another nation and that friend becomes a foe? The whole point of the economic consideration is that we should develop and support our technological expertise domestically. That is not only good business; it also serves the interests of national security. At this point, I could once again go on about the importance of creating an entrepreneurial state. However, I am certain that you have already grasped the importance of governments taking the innovative lead from earlier references in this book.

Taking the above into consideration, it is essential that we find the balance between seemingly disparate (and perhaps even contradictory) interests. The need to reach this point of shared consensus is why the principles behind sourcing relationships as opposed to deals—which are also the fundamental tenets of the Relational Model™—are critical.

We all lose if we make a decision that focuses solely on the economic gain at the expense of military requirements. Conversely, if we ignore or forfeit economic interests how can we say we served the best interests of all stakeholders?

Our previous experience with the F-35 is the reason why the relationship table of this complex acquisition should include proactive representation from the military.

Vendor Involvement

Under a static performance-based contracting process, most interaction with vendors occurs before the award of business. Once the decision has been made to do business with a particular vendor, buyers typically abdicate responsibility for the ongoing success of the acquisition only becoming involved only when the project doesn't go as planned.

This break from ongoing communication occurred in the case of the initial F-35 contract when the costs, at least according to the press, spiraled from the original $9 billion to $40 and eventually $60 billion. Based on insiders, the $9 billion was for the initial product delivery, while the $45 billion represented the total cost over the fighter's 42-year life cycle.

Regardless of the math, if the proper relational contracting model had been used to manage the relationship during and after the initial acquisition process, it is unlikely that this problem would have escalated to the point of public misinformation and embarrassment.

Whether by choice or circumstance, this does not mitigate the importance of adhering to the same relational contracting principles. Specifically, we should focus on the same critical relationship factors, including the vendor's ability to deliver on their commitment and their willingness to come to the table openly and transparently. An open and transparent environment is the only way that all stakeholders can collectively come together to identify problems before they get out of hand.

Without transparency and open communication, it's hard to come to the conclusion that the F-35 is the best solution - even if it is. Especially if ascertaining costs to which there can be a viable adherence within the agreed upon pricing model proves problematic. Or to put it another way, there is a point of negation where the fighter's benefits become outweighed by the costs of getting the required number of aircraft in the air. No matter how good the F-35 might be, if we can only afford to acquire a limited number, this will certainly not meet Canada's military needs.

That is why it is important to source the right relationships with the right vendors. Even if we use the Relational Model™ industry analytical tools and vendor capability assessments methods to identify pricing issues with the F-35 before the award of a contract, open collaboration between all stakeholders including deputy ministers, military personnel and vendors are essential to keep the relationship on track.

So, what can we do?

In this chapter, I used the F-35 case to demonstrate the size of the challenge we face in alignment or rather re-alignment of our system of checks and balances. This case illustrates the complexity and challenges governments face when aligning desired acquisition outcomes with diverse stakeholder interests.

Pickup any newspaper in the world and you read headlines announcing that yet another procurement initiative has gone off the rails. These reports of failed acquisition outcomes are not limited to the public sector.

A senior executive from a Fortune 500 company once shared details with me regarding her own organization's failure to successfully launch an ERP reverse auction program. She pointed out that the only difference between the public and private sector is that when the private sector experiences a setback, it is not likely to end up on the front page of the local paper.

As illustrated in Figure 11 below, there are many checks and balances in place within the public sector intended to protect against the disconnects that lead to challenges such as with the F-35 acquisition. However, these checks and balances are for the most part indicative of a siloed view of the procurement process in which transactional results take priority over relational outcomes.

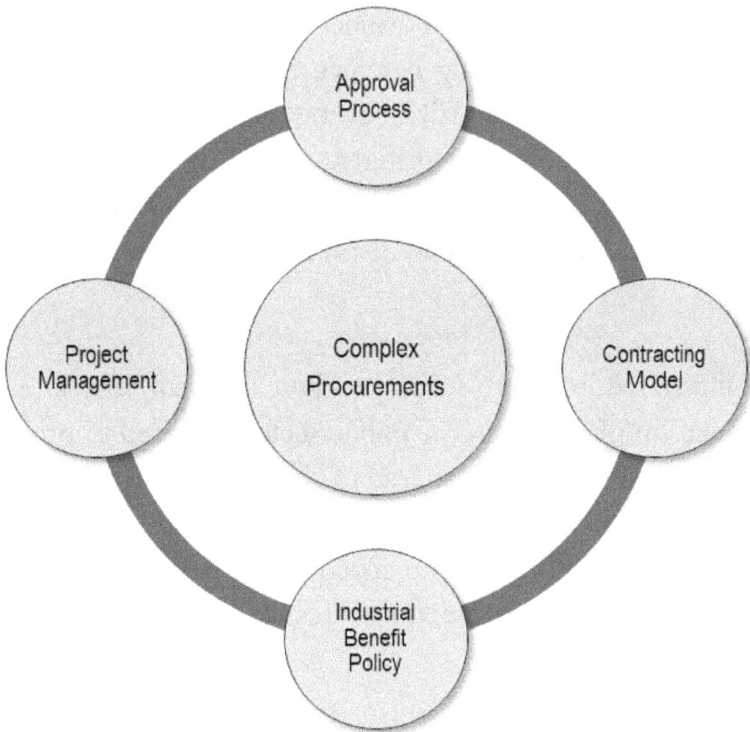

Figure 11: The Complex Procurement Cycle

Instead of attempting to legislate transactional results, we must actively partner towards relational success. Within this relational context, there needs to be a redefinition of the existing acquisition framework for complex procurements that aligns with the Pillars of the Relationship Charter.

The Approval Processes

Based on a project-oriented rather than a relationship-oriented framework, present-day public sector project approval policies are inherently transactional.

As a result, most projects are "planned or sourced" on the premise that it is possible to identify needs at a pre-determined static cost. Once a vendor has been selected, all that remains is to manage the delivery of performance milestones. However, unlike buying a pencil, complex acquisitions are subject to both known and unknown real-world variables that can impact the original contracting terms.

Why did the acquisition price for the F-35 fighter jet increase several times from an expected $9 billion to $40 and then $60 billion?

The answer is simple, we just did not know what the price tag actually is. As we gained more insight it became apparent that envisaged costs were underestimated. The problem is not in the estimate being wrong due to many unknowns, but with lack of transparency, openness, and the mindset of trying to prove and achieve certainty based on an initial set of parameters and assumptions.

Rather than providing transactional approvals under what ultimately becomes an adversarial model, governments must identify the critical relational elements that ensure ongoing collaboration and transparency that lead to the establishment of a shared mission and vision.

It is upon the principle of a shared mission and vision (the First Pillar of the Relationship Charter) that both public and private sector organizations can seek certainty in establishing and adhering to a fixed price point.

It is important to understand that this should not be confused with a blank cheque approach where running over budget becomes the norm.

Author's Notes

In truth, especially as it relates to future-sourcing contracts in which neither the buyer nor the vendor has any experience, the budget target is not and never has been a real-world number.

Forcing a set price for an undeveloped solution or service is a recipe for failure because meeting the unrealistic target will inevitably shift the focus from the desired results.

Instead, the best approach is to select the right relationship as opposed to price and then collaboratively work towards an affordable outcome within a transparently adaptable relationship model. The successful I-35 bridge project in Minnesota provides just one excellent example of the effectiveness of this approach.

Project Management

Under the traditional procurement model, the role of the Project Management Office (PMO) is to manage certainty and eliminate uncertainty. While many project managers may bristle at this suggestion, perceiving it as a lawyer's view, the reality is that contracts represent a scrutinizing belt with suspenders safety net. In my experience, relying on snapped suspenders and tightened belts, is reminiscent of the Far Side cartoon in which snake parents are bemoaning the fact that they cannot keep their sizable brood confined to an old-fashioned, wooden-barred playpen. In other words, there are just too many variables in the real world to "confine" a project to a single set of static parameters.

A legalistic approach is particularly problematic considering the fact that most projects managed by PMOs are only one component of an overall multi-faceted initiative. Think of it in terms of running a relay race. A runner can only focus on the leg of the race that he or she runs. While one runner may perform exceptionally, another may stumble, and the result is a lost race.

One of the fundamental limitations of transactional management models is that there is virtually no way for runners (stakeholders) to look beyond their "own" project. This limited view means that they are unable to collectively identify and collaboratively address the inevitable challenges that can (and will) impact a complex acquisition program.

To address these interaction barriers, it is essential that there is a mechanism in place above the individual PMO that performs this function at the relationship level rather than the project level. The Canadian government is trying to use procurement secretariats to carry out this function, such as the case with the Shipbuilding Procurement Secretariat. However, these entities are only set-up to conduct the procurement only and not to manage the delivery and life cycle of the relationship.

The Joint Governance Pillar of the Relationship Charter discussed in Section II of this book offers a framework for strategic planning and benefits realization at the "relationship" level across the silos of project management responsibility.

Industrial Technology Benefits/Value Proposition Policy

As discussed earlier in this chapter, economic imperatives must be considered from the standpoint of leveraging spending to drive broad societal benefits or offsets. The merits of linking social benefits to a significant acquisition cannot be argued, however, the means by which these benefits are realized has proven to be problematic. Vendors are often allowed to establish large offset debt and lack an immediate plan for how they will ultimately deliver—if at all.

The inability to deliver on commitments or banking obligations clearly demonstrates the mindset that promotes "win the business first at all cost, and worry about performing afterward." I lament this mindset throughout this book.

There are many reasons why promised industrial or economic benefits fail to materialize. For example, a cost model used by a vendor to win a contract may not be viable, not only for that particular vendor, but also for all vendors in the sector. As a result, financial strains may limit the viability of leveraging a regional industrial capability that could provide needed jobs.

Meeting contract deliverables when faced with declining profits or outright losses, may force vendors to seek offshore solutions at much lower costs. The risk of vendors finding themselves in this kind of position is the reason why (as highlighted in the Approval Process section, page 153) attempting to gain certainty through a fixed pricing model never works.

By using a proper industry and strategic grouping analysis, buyers are aware of when pricing expectations place an onerous burden on the market. With the focus shifting to contracting a relationship, open book policies can be established and managed to ensure that vendors realize the necessary level of profitability and fulfill broader economic policy objectives.

However, it is important to point out that governments must not rely solely on the acquisition process to drive innovation and economic growth.

Once again, referencing their 2002 report *Developing Country Firms in the World Economy: Governance and Upgrading in Global Value Chains* [vii] & [xxii], John Humphrey and Hubert Schmitz point out that relationships and relationship governance are key drivers for sector development.

It is worth repeating that it was Humphrey and Schmitz's position that "value chain research focuses on the nature of the relationships between the various actors involved in the chain, and on their implications for development." In this regard, they emphasized that governance is an essential element of a value chain and coordination is required "to take decisions not only on *what* should be, or *how* something should be produced but sometimes also *when*, and *how much* and even at *what price*."

While coordination may occur through arm's-length market relations or non-market relationships, the latter are most applicable to government procurement practices.

Humphrey and Schmitz identify the following three possible types of governance models in non-market relationships;

a) network implying cooperation between firms of more or less equal power that share their competencies within the chain;

b) quasi-hierarchy involving relationships between legally independent firms in which one is subordinate to the other, with a leader in the chain defining the rules to which the rest of the actors have to comply and

c) hierarchy when a firm is owned by an "external" firm.

The network mechanism makes the most sense from a national or "domestic" public sector procurement standpoint only if the more traditional government hierarchy mindset can reconcile itself with an implied equality of power.

As discussed in an earlier chapter, the following excerpt reiterates how this governance structure has succeeded within the software industry in China.

In their book *Clusters Facing Competition: The Importance of External Linkages* (Giuliani, Rabellotti and van Dijk, 2005), Pieter van Dijk and Quanscheng Wang highlight the collaborative process that exists between public and private sector stakeholders. They state that "software companies express what they expect from the government and local government, eager to promote the sector, is very willing to act upon their suggestions." The high level of collaborative interaction is demonstrated when local authorities "push relations with universities and local research and development institutes." This represents a pattern of governance that is commensurate with a "network type" structure.

To participate and compete in the emerging global economy, countries such as Canada and the United States must take note of the attitudes and actions of China as well as other world-stage players such as the European Association of Development Research and Training Institutes. By doing so, they will better understand that the development and utilization of indigenous or domestic clusters (which mostly comprise of SMEs) is a key tenet of building success on a global basis.

According to van Dijk and Wang, by focusing on this "interaction between internal clusters and external linkages," governments will be able to determine "how these interactions will help SMEs to face increasing global competition."

Given that offsets policy has also fallen victim to a transactional mentality. One alternative is a direct government investment in the R&D and economic activity outside the pricing model of the contract. Also, Procurement is not always the right method for stimulating and developing value in the local supply chain. Other relationships need to occur.

Knowledge and technology transfer continue to be "constrained" by factors including government red tape and competitive positioning. For that reason, procurement is not always the right strategy to create and sustain innovation. That said, through industry analysis and functional capability assessment, these factors can be identified by procurement early in the process to allow for adjustments in approach and implementation.

The Failure Of The Procurement Regime

As I have emphasized throughout this book, the primary reason that the public and private sector procurement and complex acquisition processes fail is that they emphasize sourcing transactions or deals as opposed to relationships.

This failure of the regime stems from the inability of the traditional model to view acquisitions and relationships above and beyond a single identifiable project. The inevitable result is a siloed approach that obfuscates the broader or collective goal of the total acquisition strategy. For example, a company may be adept at delivering a product from its current assembly line but still lack the capacity to manage the network of SMEs, academia and other key stakeholders to meet its offset's commitments.

In instances such as this collaborative makeup and will of an organization comes into play.

An ISM, CAPS and A.T. Kearney report released in May 2007,[xxxv] identified internal and external collaboration as a critical component of a successful procurement regime. The report emphasized that "to extract the significant gains that collaboration can bring, companies will need to enable best-practice multi-lateral collaboration between supply partners, achieve integrated product development, and employ *customer of choice* positioning."

I could not agree more with the study's position on collaboration.

Internal government collaboration through the sourcing of relationships needs to occur using a cross-department, cross-agency collaborative framework that empowers interagency or interdepartmental accountability. This broad framework will, in turn, facilitate horizontal strategic planning that will align with the decision-making process.

Once the internal collaboration model has been set, the framework should be extended to include vendor relationships.

The key to a successful collaboration with vendors is to accurately assess and evaluate on an ongoing basis their ability to deliver all the expected outcomes of an initiative.

It is within this collaborative context that the Relational Model™ industry analysis tools are so important, as represented by the Fourth and final Pillar of The Relationship Charter–Ongoing Stakeholder Viability.

Summary of the main areas of action

1. **Approval Policy**: The approval policy must shift approval measurements from estimates to relationships, and interdepartmental governance.

2. **Project Management**: Project management must gain a broader, enterprise-wide understanding of how particular projects integrate with and impact the "collective" objectives of a complex acquisition.

3. **Industrial Benefits**: The procurement system needs to assess better whether the industry can meet objectives, and if not, find alternate methods (other than procurement) to build an endowment and sustained economic value.

4. **Procurement Regime**: Improved internal and external collaboration is needed to establish effective procurement strategies and to source and manage relationships.

Considering sustainable value is a good starting point for any complex acquisition within the public and the private sector, it is important to note that success is not limited to one stream of thought.

We cannot serve the needs of a single stakeholder without taking into account the collective interests of all stakeholders.

Chapter 10

Are You Ready To Become Relational?

Over the past couple of years, there has been a notable shift in the area of complex business arrangements that include outsourcing, public-public partnership, and public-private partnerships. The central theme with each of these is the increasing focus on the importance of relationships. Specifically, the recognition that the effective management of the relationship between all stakeholders is the single most critical element of a successful initiative.

Even industry associations and practitioners of transformational and vested outsourcing are now talking about relational importance as they transition their models towards what I call a Relationship First approach.

The introduction of the new ISO 44001 standard that I have talked about earlier in this book and will review in greater detail later in this chapter also mirrors the fundamental elements of the Relational Model™. In fact, and given my direct involvement with its introduction into Canada, it is safe to say that the Relational Model™ has left an indelible mark on ISO 44001.

So, what does it mean to be truly relational?

Before I answer that question, let's quickly identify what it isn't?

To start, terms such as win-win and the mere acknowledgment that relationships are important is not enough. The reason is that recognition without meaningful action is nothing more than wrapping the old adversarial model in shiny paper and putting a bow on it. Unfortunately, this repackaging exercise has been repeated far too often because it is much easier to add a new label to an existing model than it is to make the necessary changes to being relational—especially within the public sector. The reason for semantical observation instead of "practical" adoption is that becoming relational means that you will almost always have to facilitate a cultural shift within the organization from the top down.

For many, the prospect of a cultural change is a daunting, even fearful exercise. It forces us to shift from a familiar fixed or performance-based model that is structured around an adherence to the inflexible terms and conditions associated with a static outcome.

The main problem is that the real world does not operate within the narrowly defined conditions of a contract, no matter how well it is structured.

Initiative goals can and do change, and with it the capabilities of key stakeholders to fulfill their established role. This means that rather than attempting to enforce compliance to a rigid set of performance requirements based on a single point in time objective, one must be able to adapt to the reality of inevitable change.

The recognition and subsequent ability to adapt to changing goals and stakeholder capabilities, is the true definition of a relational arrangement.

However, to reach this point of relational readiness, it is important to build awareness and capacity within the buying organization. This kind of education process, as I will call it, must target all levels of the organization from senior executives to those who are managing the day-to-day activities. Therefore, the focus of this program should include:

1. A general understanding of the relationship-based model from the standpoint of not only its differences from transactional or performance-based models but also the corresponding benefits regarding improved outcomes. Having an understanding of the needed organizational structure, process and behavioral changes associated with being a participant in a high performing relationship are also essential.

2. A guideline for how to plan and source a relationship, as opposed to a transaction or one-time negotiated deal including; i) How to define the attributes of the required relationship, ii) How to objectively select vendor(s) based on those characteristics in a manner that satisfies the tendering process, and iii) How to build a Relationship Charter during the procurement process.

3. A process to operationalize the Relationship Charter by transforming it from a well-intentioned paper model, to one in which it reflects the way that stakeholders actually work together towards achieving a mutually beneficial improved outcome.

4. The mechanism to organize, tool and manage the partner relationships management function within the organization.

The focus of this final chapter will be to provide you with a detailed breakdown of each of the above steps. My intention is to enable you to establish and progress through a relational readiness process that empowers you to achieve desired outcomes with a Relationships First approach.

Point 1 - What Is A High Performing Business Relationship?

In the previous section, I talked about the need to move beyond the semantic definition of a business relationship to a state of relational readiness. Specifically, positioning your organization to look outside of the narrowly defined and largely ineffective performance-based contracting model, to an adaptive relational framework which focuses on improving outcomes.

A critical element of this transition begins with the recognition that both objectives and stakeholder capabilities can and frequently do change from the point of initial engagement. Recognizing the inevitability of change in complex business relationships is the first step.

Next, you must create a framework for managing these changes within the context of both existing as well as new relationships.

Taking into account the reality of changing capabilities within both existing as well as new relationships will bring your organization to the point of relational readiness.

In doing so, there are three distinct areas of focus. The first is defining the high-performance business relationship.

First, let's take the myth out of the relational terminology.

As discussed earlier in this book, Relational contract theory has been around for a long time. It simply means that the whole agreement is not necessarily within the four corners of the contract. Almost all complex contracts contain this type of provision, giving the ability to do amendments via a prescribed change order process. In this sense, everyone's model is relational.

On one extreme, you have standards that promote spending tremendous amounts of energy to define some end state, creating work statements and metrics that presumably would achieve that end state, and then sourcing a vendor that can deliver that state. I often refer to those as transaction-oriented, performance-based models. Now those deals also contain relationships and have relationship management frameworks. However, the relationship management function exists mostly to materialize "the deal" based on an initial set of assumptions and parameters. In other words, the relationship management function is really no more than another approach to enforce compliance to achieve a predetermined state or outcome.

Procurement is easy in this type of model. Technical capability and capacity to deliver a known end state (product or service) and a fixed definition of value (financial or otherwise) as perceived at the time of the transaction determines vendor selection.

When it comes to meeting stakeholder expectations, this approach usually falls short. We have already seen the consequences of these types of arrangements, particularly when they span decades. The greatest challenge is that no amount of time and expertise expended by executives, lawyers, financial modelers, program managers or procurement people can create certainty over the long life of a contract.

A relationship-based model lies exactly on the other side of this spectrum. With this model, the embodiment of a true relationship is within the SRS Relationship Charter. The Charter, which provides the operational framework for a joint organizational entity, is centered around a clearly defined mission that includes the relationship's purpose, values, supporting processes and people.

It is through this integrated joint body that the generation of deliverables, the development and continuous alignment of the relationship's strategic plan, product/service delivery and performance is managed. It is important to note that when I refer to delivery and performance management, I am not talking about vendor performance, but relationship performance. This distinction is important because when we usually talk about relationships, it is within the context of a traditional performance-based contract.

With the relationship-based model, the process for selecting a strategic partner or partners is different, as it utilizes a strategic fit assessment and financial pricing model to determine partner viability. Of course, the pricing model to which I am referring is different from that of which most are likely familiar, as it relies on dynamic cost-objects, as opposed to a predetermined set of items that define value at a certain point in time.

Recognizing and being able to adapt and leverage the inevitability of change as a strategic advantage is one of the main benefits of the relationship-based model. It is an advantage because the relationship-based model proactively channels stakeholder energies towards continuously improving the definition of the outcome and the related technical processes that ultimately generate the deliverables. In this regard, it is a dynamic and continuous process for planning, implementing, measuring, learning and problem-solving. It is also from within this type of framework that high performing relationships ultimately grow.

In reading the previous chapters in this book, you know that a high performing relationship is one that exhibits the following business process traits or elements:

- **The Act of Relating** – Connecting and linking in a natural, complementary way. Having the ability to relate is where strategic fit assessment is paramount, including the alignment of strategic direction and capabilities within the context of strategic program objectives;

- **Mutuality** – Sharing the same or similar views, ethics, outputs, each to the other;

- **Respect** – Recognizing and considering each other's needs, requirements, contributions, abilities, qualities, and achievements;

- **Innovation** – Use of combined strengths and synergies to gain insight and deliver improved outcomes;

- **Continuous Alignment** – Commitment to making the necessary adjustments to minimize risk, optimize or improve the outcomes and maximize the realization of benefits for all stakeholders;

- **Empowerment** – Introducing joint integrated management structures and processes to gain needed insight to manage risk and for managing the relationship at the strategic, tactical and operational levels.

Understanding these elements, it becomes clear that high performing relationships are all about creating high performing teams. As the inexhaustible number of case studies and reference materials over the years demonstrate, no amount of contractual structuring based upon a traditional procurement process can accomplish this objective.

Success with this new paradigm rests in our ability to change our familiar yet ineffective approach to sourcing and managing relationships. It means that we have to focus on ways to create a culture of organizational trust and collaboration, particularly within the public sector. Specifically, it's the need to see Relationships beyond a one-off deal or transaction based upon a specified need at a single, static point in time.

Of course, to attain this level of relational excellence requires a cultural change within an organization in which stakeholder teams, as I call them, share a common purpose and are driven by an ongoing alignment of capabilities.

To this end, there is a need to redefine the organization's internal vendor management and contract compliance protocols, as well as risk management oversight, before a real transformation to a high performing relationship model can occur. In short, you have to stop managing vendors and start managing relationships based on a culture of collaboration and trust.

The requirement to successfully establish or expand upon this culture within an organization is why the ISO 44001 standard (Corporate Relationship Management Plan) that I have referenced at key points throughout this book is so important as it confirms the metrics associated with the Relational Model.

Point 2 - How Do You Source A High Performing Business Relationship?

Now that we have identified what a high-performance relationship is, the next question is, how do you find one? Or perhaps the better word would be "establish" one?

"The contract must become a platform to manage inevitable change, not pursue certainty based on the original deal." ~ Ian Mack. Director General Major Project Delivery (Land & Sea), Canadian Department of National Defence

The Relational Ties That Bind

Establishing a collaborative high performing relationship requires a different set of activities within the sourcing process. It requires a different additional relational activities because one cannot use the prescriptive or familiar procurement mechanisms to source a dynamic business relationship, especially with Futuresourcing™ initiatives.

With Futuresourcing™ initiatives, where neither the client nor the vendor has constructed, built or delivered the required capability, past work experience cannot be solely relied upon or used as a selection criterion.

In "sourcing" dynamic relationships, a closer examination of the vendor's strategy and core capabilities are paramount to determining the likelihood of the ultimate success of the relationship.

In this context, all projects should be viewed with this fresh look of uncertainty, especially given the fact that the vast majority have failed to deliver the expected results.

Beyond these needed checks and balances, the right sourcing process advocates an intensive industry analysis and engagement before and during the actual procurement, as well as post procurement. This sourcing process also involves the application of advanced analytical tools to objectively assess and evaluate the fit between a vendor's strategy, core capabilities and the initiative's strategic objectives relative to the expected outcome.

With high performing relationships, collaboration is born out of common purpose and intent, and must, therefore, be a product of strategic fit. The advanced analytical tools associated with the Relational Model™ are used to determine the veracity of the strategic fit between the client and vendor. This fit as I call it is critical for establishing the framework for the Relationship Charter a topic that I will continue to address in future publications.

It is important to note at this point that irrespective of where you presently are regarding your current contract management life cycle, it is never too late to introduce a relationship-based model. However, the sooner you incorporate the model in your process the sooner, you will realize all of the benefits delivered by the Relational Model™.

Within the context of the above, the following 4-Step process will enable you to source and establish high performing relationships reliably.

Step 1 – Creating The BRF™ Framework

As stated earlier, SRS had established Benefits Realization Factors (BRF™) a few years earlier as a means of defining the variables or key factors that must be enabled to achieve success relative to the expected outcome.

BRF's™ should not be confused with Key Performance Indicators (KPIs), which need to be defined jointly with your selected partner at a later stage. A BRF™ to a procurement initiative outcome is much like a Critical Success Factor (CSF) to project management and risk factor in risk management.

To have "meaning" it is a factor that enables the desired benefits associated with an acquisition or delivery. In this context, and as mentioned earlier in the book, I am confident that almost all procurement professionals can recall at least one initiative where despite the presence of one or two success factors, there wasn't a realization of the expected outcome regarding the overall initiative.

Step 2 – Industry analysis

The questions I am most frequently asked relate to the advanced analytical tools I use to understand an industry and assess the strategic fit between potential partners.

The fundamental idea behind the utilization of these tools is to introduce Competitive Analysis and Competitive Intelligence gathering within a procurement framework, before the actual procurement itself. These tools ultimately enhance both the insight and the understanding of specific organizations within those industries, as well as the industry as a whole to identify better the critical points of strategic fit relative to achieving an expected or desired outcome.

This initial step, in essence, provides an understanding of an industry as opposed to an individual company. By using a single standard that aligns with your contracting goals, you are in a better position to compare all competitive bidder capabilities.

Or to put it another way, to understand individual company capabilities, you must first know what their particular industry is doing as a whole. It is at this point that the importance of strategic grouping comes into play.

A strategic group is a concept used in strategic management that groups companies within an industry with similar business models or similar combinations of strategies.

My Strategic Group Analysis (SGA) aims to identify organizations with similar strategic characteristics, following similar strategies or competing on a somewhat similar basis.

The Industry Analysis phase also provides added insight needed in your procurement strategy, enabling you to determine if your expected outcomes and BRF™ are achievable.

This second step establishes the preliminary alignment between your objectives and industry capabilities that enable you to engage the targeted industry intelligently.

Step 3 – Strategy And Industry Engagement

One of the critical issues engulfing the procurement regimes particularly in the public sector is "industry engagement." For many years, the government only relied on defining their requirements and then taking them to market in the hope that a vendor, any vendor would be able to step forward and deliver to contract specifications.

The problem with this approach is that it abdicates buyer responsibility regarding the successful delivery of the required product or service. In essence, the government would ask for A and then rely on imposing legal terminology and financial penalties as a means of enforcing the desired outcome.

History has demonstrated that this approach in both the public and private sectors has failed to produce satisfactory results.

With Steps 1 and 2, we have addressed this issue.

Based on your newly gained insight of the industry, rather than raising the defined requirement flag in the hope that a vendor, any vendor, will salute it, you are now able to develop a strategy that focuses on two key elements.

The first element is the business arrangement framework, which includes a description of your strategic objectives and the resulting alignment with target industry capabilities. From this, the profile for an ideal business arrangement that encompasses the actual relationship itself, as well as the corresponding service and financial management framework, will emerge.

Once you know what you require in a high performing relationship partner or partners, the second element, which is a description of the procurement process itself, can be mapped out and implemented.

It is important to note that this initial connecting point with the target industry is part of an ongoing engagement process, that will continue to provide intelligence to what will become the joint governance team, throughout the relationship. I will talk about joint governance in greater detail later when I review the process to operationalize the Relationship Charter.

In the meantime, we are now ready to move on to the fourth and final step in sourcing a high performing relationship.

Step 4 – Vendor Selection

In sourcing high performing relationships, vendor selection is based primarily on the following four components:

1. A business proposal that describes the general approach and strategy for meeting known deliverables and immediate or short-term goals, along with any technical, HR and management plans that may be required in the short term as seen and determined by the bidder.

2. Strategic Fit Assessment – As mentioned earlier in this section, this is a process that uses advanced analytical tools to objectively quantify the fit between a corporate strategy and core capabilities, with BRF™. The assessment output is what we call a Relationship Certainty Score and is carried out by an independent team of qualified professionals in strategy, finance, and business operations.

3. Relationship Charter components and Joint Governance team qualifications. The introduction of the Relationship Charter during the procurement process (components of which will be covered later when I review Operationalizing the Relationship

Charter) will be in a Straw model template format. The Relationship Charter, finalized at the negotiation phase of the procurement, is one of the few things that will require phase-based negation in the relational approach.

4. Open book framework, which is the information management and financial evaluation of vendors proposed financial terms and management metrics. As previously mentioned, the OBF is a pricing model based on actual cost accounting with dynamic constructs and incentives depending on the type of activities involved during the relation- ship life cycle.

5. Last but not least, and before any transition can take place, operationalizing the Relationship Charter is critical as it empowers stakeholders to work in teams as a cohesive single unit. This collaborative cohesion is at the heart of any high performing strategic relationship, and it is the Charter platform that provides the parties with the ability to efficiently and successfully address problem areas as they arise, as opposed to being avoided. This Charter platform also provides the insight into the relationship elements that enables the delivery of improved outcomes and the intelligence across the value chain to better leverage change as a strategic advantage as opposed to being viewed as an undesired and unanticipated risk. As a result, there is a resiliency to the relationship in times

of inevitable change that ensures an efficient shared response, and ultimately a successful outcome.

In the next section, I will go into greater detail regarding how to operationalize the Relationship Charter. However, the following response to a question a senior private sector executive gave when asked why relationship-based models work, is the key takeaway from this section:

> *"Successful private sector organizations attribute their success to close customer intimacy where they learn and work with their clients to produce the next generation products and services— the relationship based model is the systematic approach that delivers customer intimacy."*

Point 3 - Converting Knowledge Into Sustainable Action

I remember once reading an article, which talked about the fact that businesses spend far more time and money on training programs that do not ultimately deliver, develop or demonstrate long-term results.

The article went on to say that "to make new behaviors sustaining, you have to translate knowledge into committed action." In short, if there is to be an actual investment payback, training "must endure beyond a moment in time insight," and "inspire and empower ongoing action through practical application."

The above sums up entirely the enduring principles behind the creation and operationalization of the Relationship Charter.

As a fundamental tenet of the Relational Model™, the Relationship Charter provides a collaborative framework that defines the relationship, its method of planning and operational management activities. At its core, it is a living document.

The focus of this third section of the chapter, "Are You Ready To Become Relational," provides you with the tools to both establish and operationalize your Relationship Charter.

Establishing The Relationship Charter Foundation For Success

When I talk about establishing the Relationship Charter, I am referring to its development and finalization.

Establishing the charter is reflective of a collaborative process in which this foundation for the post-contract award relationship is co-developed during the procurement or sourcing, as well as the onboarding stage of a complex acquisition. Specifically, with the establishment of the short list of vendors, they would, as part of the proposal submission and evaluation phase, be provided with a charter straw model template that reflects relational principles, values, joint governance and open book framework.

The completion of the template will serve as a means of soliciting initial partner input in which the information will determine the relational fit between a prospective vendor and the buying organization.

The straw model template is a critical element of the complex acquisition process in that it will either confirm the relational compatibility between the buyer and vendor or identify potential areas of possible disconnect that require further clarification and a corrective course of action.

After addressing the areas of disconnect, and a partner is selected, the cooperative charter development process transitions through the negotiation and onboarding phase. It is at this next stage that a joint collaborative engagement is undertaken to complete or finalize the charter's components and operational management structures. It does so, taking into account the existing partners' capacities and abilities, as well as those of the new partners or consortia members.

For many, the proactive and forward-looking identification of potential issues that can negatively impact the success of the initiative in a genuinely probative manner is both new and somewhat revolutionary. Calling on, once again, the long journey analogy I used in a previous section, while it is important to make certain that your car is in tip-top shape before you take to the road, thereby reducing the risk of a breakdown, you also need a contingency capability should something unexpected happen.

In this context, the charter template exercise serves two important purposes; 1) to make certain that you select the right partner based on what you know today and, 2) to make sure you have the right partner in terms of their ability to work collaboratively with you so you can adapt to an unforeseen situation that neither buyer nor vendor could have reasonably anticipated.

Operationalizing The Relationship Charter

When I talk about operationalizing, what I am referring to is bringing the charter itself to life through a broader engagement of all stakeholders, including everyone who is involved in the management and operational processes associated with the initiative.

For greater clarity, although the Relationship Charter is developed through a collaborative engagement process, its operationalization is the step that transforms the it from being a paper model to one that orchestrates a series of coordinated human interactions towards achieving relationship objectives.

Generally speaking, the establishment and operationalization process involves three major steps:

1. **Orientation** – introduce stakeholder teams and all those who are affected by the relationship, to the relationship-based model, including the relationship

charter components, and how to work in teams. This process usually involves team exercises in charter development, team relationships strengthening and working collaboratively.

2. **Joint** Workshops – understand, internalize and further refine the charter components including mission, vision, values, goals, joint governance primary and tertiary structures, and the financial management framework. It is also through these workshops that performance, risk and enablement strategies and metrics, change management strategies, broader stakeholder engagement, competency development and information sharing takes place. Strategic and operational planning teams and processes are kicked off at this stage.

3. **Validation and Learning** – summarize the results of the operationalization process as a means of verifying learning, commitments, and collaborative behaviors. This step also involves lessons-learned sessions, as well as improvement plan design for future implementations.

Notwithstanding the above, and referencing this chapter's first section, I had indicated that everyone's model contains some relational elements. In other words, we all need to manage a relationship or relationships regardless of the original framework through which the participating stakeholders came together and the corresponding objectives established.

Whether your present model is transactional, performance-based or a derivative of the two, you need to operationalize your relationships using the same steps I have outlined above, particularly in the context of your present deal or transaction.

As previously stressed, it is obviously more advantageous to establish the Relationship Charter through the planning and procurement or sourcing stage. However, if you are working with an existing contract, operationalization becomes even more critical. My experience over the past 25 years has demonstrated that the failure to operationalize a relationship almost always leads to an adversarial culture that manifests itself in one form or another between the primary stakeholders. This manifestation ultimately results in what I have commonly referred to as being the contract divide, in which individual stakeholders begin focusing on a self-serving agenda.

In my next and final section of this chapter, I talk about the steps you will have to take to ensure that your organization is ready to be part of a collaborative relationship.

Point 4 - Achieving Certainty: How To Create A Culture Of Collaboration

The sole purpose of setting up a contract is to establish a "path of certainty" that guarantees a successful outcome. In short, if I do A and you do B we should achieve C.

Unfortunately, there is no such thing as absolute certainty

in the real world. As a result, even a well-crafted contract with clearly defined terms and conditions fails if it does not accommodate the need to adapt to the inevitable changes that occur over the life of the agreement.

When I talk about changes and adaptability, I am not referring to compliance relating to the terms of the contract itself. I am speaking about the practicality of recognizing and responding to previously unidentified external factors that were not part of the original contract, and therefore, fall outside of the framework of the existing agreement.

Once again, and using my long journey analogy, you may have chosen a particular route to get from one place to another, based upon known factors such as distance and time. In this regard, you anticipate the length of time you are on the road, and at what points you have to stop along the way to refuel.

But what happens if during the actual journey you encounter inclement weather? What if you discover that the route you had originally planned to take has an unexpected detour or you experience car trouble. What do you do?
You adapt.

For example, with inclement weather, you likely delay your journey and spend time at a rest stop along the way until it blows over. This delay may mean that you take longer than expected to arrive at your destination but you ultimately arrive safe and sound.

Seems simple enough. Even though you did not expect to encounter severe weather when it hit, rather than pushing through with potentially dire consequences to adhere to the original plan, you adapted to a new reality or set of circumstances.

This level of adaptability to changing conditions demonstrates both experience and maturity.

Within the context of a contract, there is usually little if any room for such flexibility. The reason is that we are locked into its terms, even if said terms do not reflect the unexpected events of the real world. In those instances, where one party is late on a deliverable due to unforeseen circumstances, they are more likely to be penalized, even if said delay benefits the entire project in the long run.

As a result, using contracts to manage relationships does not reflect relational maturity.

What Is Relational Maturity?

Relational maturity in its most elemental form is present when there is a desire on the part of all stakeholders to participate as productive and useful partners in a long-term arrangement. However, it is imperative that we extend ourselves beyond a mere desire to be relational through the creation and establishment of a stable yet robust management structure within a truly collaborative organizational culture.

In other words, the relationally mature organization takes a different approach. It abandons the practice of employing a top-down command and control model of management in which there are thick layers of oversight centered around a compliance management approach that reflect a contract enforcement mentality. The relationally mature organization includes recognizing and responding to change from the standpoint of achieving the best outcome, even if said change means expanding upon the original engagement parameters.

With the relationally mature organization, such expansions or adjustments do not occur through an onerous change management process. Nor are partners exposed to penalization if they acknowledge the rise of unanticipated issues.

Instead, a relationally mature organization, which has established the necessary systems and processes to facilitate the collaborative approach to problem-solving, can proactively manage change while keeping the desired outcome clearly in site. Similar to Jim Collins' autopsies with blame approach, which he identified as being one of the key differentiators with the companies who have made the transition from good to great, the relationally mature organization seeks solutions as opposed to either assigning blame or enforcing adherence to terms and conditions that are no longer relevant.

A new model of engagement is needed to get to this point of productive partnering or relational maturity.

Corporate Relationship Management Plan

The Relational Model™ to which I have referred throughout this book centers around the core concept of establishing a charter that becomes the strategic and operational framework for the relationship.

Reflecting the main elements of the new ISO 44001 standard the Relational Model™ charter provides an internationally recognized framework for managing complex business arrangements on a global basis through the establishment of a collaborative relationship plan.

While it represents a departure from how we have traditionally viewed relationship sourcing and management, which in the past has been based primarily on a contract compliance or enforcement mechanism, it is nonetheless reflective of a paradigm shift in the way we do business.

Even though changing a company's culture is not an easy task, it is nevertheless essential for success. To overcome the inevitable resistance to change means that the internal organization (Program Owner), as well as the partner's or partners' service capabilities, need to be properly aligned and enabled for the joint relationship structure to work. By this, I mean that on the one hand, a mechanism is required to translate business objectives and priorities into performance goals for the relationship. On the other hand, there is the need to support and process relationship requirements and take the necessary measures to enable them.

The primary internal organizational framework needed for effective relationship delivery management as well as operationalizing the ISO 44001 standard involves establishing and operationalizing the following management structures:

- **Relationship Approval and Review Board (RARB)** – an executive committee representing lines of business, procurement, delivery, finance and legally responsible for achieving corporate objectives through strategic relationships. RARB satisfies the Senior Executive Responsible requirement under ISO 44001.

- **Relationship and Delivery Management function (RDM)** – an organization reporting to the RARB responsible for the administration of the relational approach including, but not limited to, standards, coaching, joint governance secretariat, change management, relationships budgeting process, operational reviews and relationships portfolio management.

From an implementation perspective, there are two ways one can establish an RDM function:

- Owner of Relationships and Service Delivery Management under a subcontract from the lines of business, having accountability for delivering on relationships performance objectives at the individual as well as the relationships portfolio levels; or

- As a Centre of Excellence where the group provides advisory support, establishes standards, processes and templates for RDM function and, as well, provides advisory services and value analysis to the lines of business.

A mini RDM function is sometimes structured to support a single program with multiple strategic relationships. In that case, we refer to it as RMO or Relationships and delivery Management Office which in addition to its RDM role, it manages the operations of the joint governance system and its processes for all relationships involved.

Relationship and Delivery Management Function Implementation

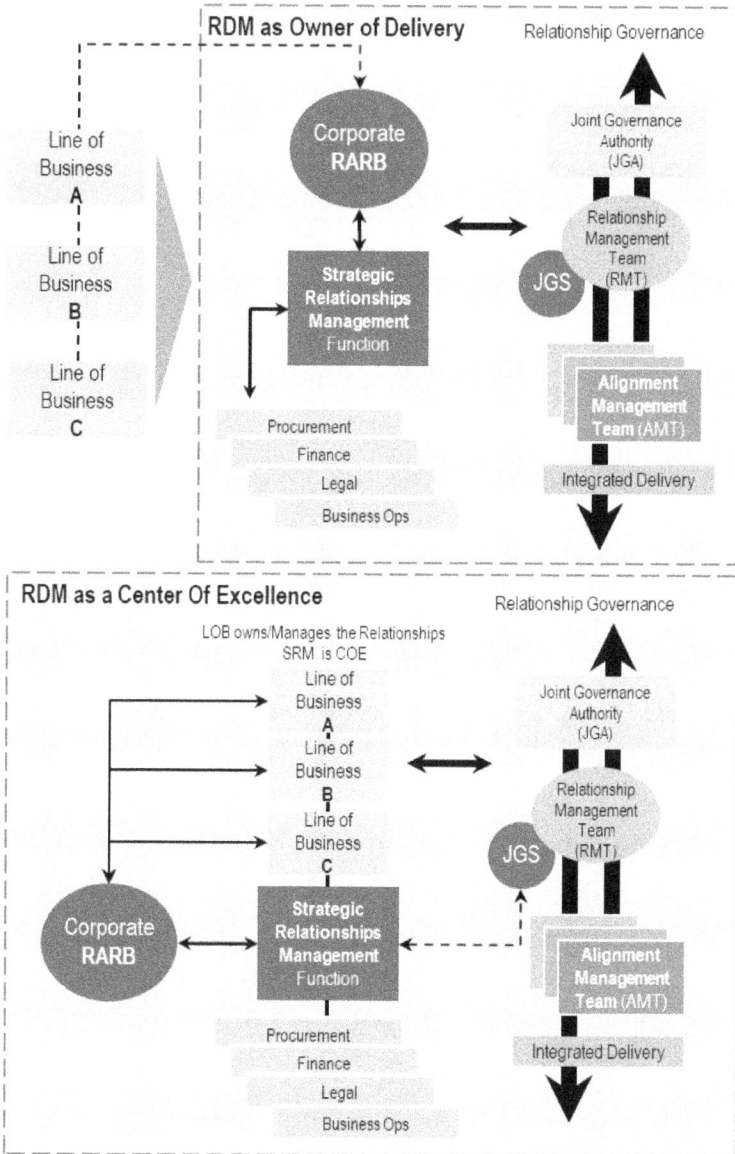

Figure 12: An example of Relationship and Delivery Management Function Implementation

Even though complex business arrangements are intricate and diverse, beyond this basic management structure success is ultimately based on people. More to the point, people working together to achieve a mutually beneficial goal within an operational framework of shared values and open dialogue. As such, becoming relationally mature is a journey that requires the presence of the following key elements:

- **Leadership** – recognition at the executive table that delivery models of today rely on partner capabilities, which include a high degree of agility and responsiveness that is only possible through adaptive and collaborative relationships as opposed to transactions or deals.

- **Business Operations** – proactive implementation of the model, which includes the institution of the RARB, RDM/RMO and the Relational Governance structures as referenced.

- **Education** – continuous education programs for individuals involved both directly and indirectly with the initiative to ensure that the structures and processes to facilitate the creation of high performing relationships are understood.

- **Incentives** – establishing incentive-based HR programs to promote collaborative behavior within the organization and across all participating organizations.

- **Communication** – a relentless communication program supported by substantive and continuous messaging from the top.

Epilogue

In the first part of this book, I talked about the important role that key individuals played in the successful implementation of the Relational Model™—particularly in its early years.

As the first executives to use the Relational Model™ in a real-world environment, both Raymond Picard and Normand Labbare, the CIO for the Museum of Nature helped to lay a solid foundation for the management of complex contracts.

TransAlta's CIO Gary Moore ignited the spark that led to the model's baptism by fire as I called it. Moore challenged us to test its value principles, which was important in that as fire purifies steel to make it stronger, the TransAlta challenge helped to solidify the model's value approach by demonstrating that it could successfully turn around the fortunes of an existing contract.

Of course, the list of individuals who both individually and collectively helped to shape the Relational Model™ over the years is long. It is within the framework of this genealogy of experience and experiences that the real value of the Relational Model™ resides.

While every initiative undoubtedly requires a champion, at some point for it to succeed, the model itself must become self-sustaining.

In other words, the relational values of the model must be interwoven into the culture of the organizations and reflected in the shared values and collaborative efforts of its people. Specifically, there has to be an element or elements of consistent values that transcend situational requirements and changing circumstances.

Unless the parties to a complex agreement believe in and ultimately adopt the underlying values of the relationship, there will be a continuous need to champion the cause within a contractual framework. In this latter scenario, active collaboration cedes to the enforcement of terms and conditions. As a result, the reliance on contracts to instill the "necessary" shared values into the relationship for it to be successful has time and again proven to be inadequate and largely ineffectual.

In this context, even though situations and requirements will, over the life of a relationship, change, success is based on the shared and unchanging values of all stakeholders. It is this commonality of values that is the central and enduring tenet of the Relational Model™.

Where We Are Today

Even though terms such as win-win and the emphasis on the importance of relationships are nothing new, what has changed in recent years is the recognition that merely expressing the desire to be relational is not enough. There has to be a defined plan to follow, a road map for building relationships that produce results.

Given this changed climate of relational understanding, the model referenced throughout this book provides the steps that an organization or organizations must take to put relationships first.

Putting relationships first does not mean that I am advocating the abolishment of contracts or transactions. As discussed in this book, contracts have an obvious and no less important role to play in transactional, short-term arrangements.

However, and as I had indicated in the third chapter, "traditional contracts are based on a static governance model that is the epitome of inflexibility." The model by which I had overseen the Museum and TransAlta accounts required what I referred to as active management. They were not just "sign and forget about it" arrangements between two separate and distinct entities only to be called upon when there was a missed deliverable, or a violated term or condition.

A Relational Model™ - a real "Relational Model" does require ongoing involvement to achieve the desired results.

Years ago, a requirement for this level of engagement was usually met with surprise if not dismissed outright. After all, "if we have a contract, it is up to the vendor to deliver" was the common refrain. Attitudes, of course, changed when all parties equally felt the consequences of a failing or failed initiative. At that point, having a contract towards which you could readily cite the terms and conditions was tantamount to a Pyrrhic victory. In short, no one won, and everybody lost and lost big!

As a result, and it has taken time, the desire for a better way of managing complex relationships (and contracts) has entered mainstream thinking.

The timing for this book and the model to which it refers could not be better.

By reading this book and taking my seminars, you will position yourself as an industry expert on the way that business will be done going forward; putting Relationships First!

Afterword

This book has provided a detailed and very personal account of my experience in shepherding the development of the Relational Business Model™, a framework that can help organizations manage relationships as opposed to transactions or deals.

I have used a variety of public and private sector examples and cited a broad range of experts to illustrate how this unique and efficient model has proven its value throughout the years during many different political and economic circumstances.

It has indeed been a long and winding road, but I am confident that the Relational Model™ provides a new paradigm that will result in more insight and meaningful oversight, and ensure that governments and corporations can achieve a strategic relational alignment.

Real contracting success will remain elusive as long as public and private sector organizations continue to rely on outsourcing partners who provide services based on a static requirement from a single, specific point in time.

The Relational Model™ represents a new paradigm of thinking and managing complex business relationships. It is my sincere hope that this book will help you and your organization identify with and better understand the fundamental tenants of the Relational Model™ so you can implement the model on a level that is most relevant to your unique situations and circumstances.

Appendix A

Hypothetical Case Study A (Part 1)

Provincial and federal authorities are considering a new electromagnetic train to increase commerce between the cities of Montreal, Ottawa, and Toronto. Average travel time between the centers is expected to be almost the same as air travel. An advisory firm has recommended partnering with the private sector to carry out this project, and an initial study has indicated that several major firms have the ability to build and operate the trains.

QUESTION:

Which of the following options would be considered a viable strategy that could deliver a high degree of service availability and consumer protection against future pricing?

1. FutureSource™, e.g. contract the building of the new trains and have existing lines manage the operations of new trains.
2. Outsource existing operations to save money in the short term and Futuresource™ the new trains and the operations.
3. Privatize it completely. Sell the right to operate a new line of service/trains to the private sector and decommission existing lines.

4. PP-P – Have the private sector build and operate the trains under a dynamic shared risk and reward model.

ANSWERS:

1. FutureSourcing™ is an excellent way to build the new infrastructure and use current employees. It requires training and knowledge transfer and could provide knowledge gained through many years of managing existing operations.
2. Outsourcing and Futuresourcing™ the new trains and the new operations would separate the new and the old. In this case, the authorities would need to manage "bringing in" the new service and decommissioning the old one. There may be more job losses in this scenario.
3. Privatize it completely. Privatization would involve selling Via Rail to the private sector with a schedule for renewal and pricing based on building and operating the new trains.
4. PP-P – This option would take advantage of private sector capability to build and operate the new service. The government would decommission existing passenger service (a variation of 2 above). However, there would be stronger governance that allows for changes in the allocation of the risk and reward.

All are viable strategies, and each has its pros and cons based on past implementations. (Personally, I prefer Strategy 4.)

Let's say that the authorities decide to adopt a build/operate/transfer) approach. The leading proposal offers the provinces an upfront $3 billion in much-needed cash and $1 million per year in administration support fees. There would also be a limitation of $0.3 per kilometer traveled (indexed for inflation) for the duration of the 25-year concession agreement.

These prices are one-quarter of what it currently costs to travel by airline. The operator would have a five-year federal and provincial tax "holiday" starting the first year of operation, followed by an accelerated depreciation schedule.

QUESTIONS:

Under the above scenario, which of the following are key concerns?

1. Consumer protection
2. Fixed fee schedule
3. Cap on government revenue
4. Creating a monopoly
5. Impact on the airline industry
6. Safety

Who do you think would disproportionately benefit most from this arrangement in the long term?

1. The governments which are party to the arrangement
2. The operator

3. The users of the service
4. No one knows

ANSWER:

All are key issues. The chosen strategy is a transactional type of deal.

QUESTION:

Who do you think would disproportionately benefit most from this arrangement in the long term?

1. The governments which are party to the arrangement
2. The operator (private sector consortia)
3. The users of the service
4. No one knows

ANSWER:

More than likely it is the operator who would benefit most.

In fact, all project assumptions would be in favor of the operator. A sovereignty clause or service purchase agreement or other forms of guarantees are mandated depending on the country and economic conditions.

Hypothetical Case Study A (Part 2)

With the analysis and planning for the new electromagnetic train, federal authorities raise serious concerns about the structure of the proposed transaction and retain a second advisory firm who recommends the use of a relational approach to mitigate risk and as a way of rewarding all parties while protecting consumers. The relationship management and financial structure adhere to the following relational principles:

1. An open book revenue sharing financial management framework where:
   - The provinces would receive an initial cash payment of $3 billion.
   - The fee schedule would be dynamic but initially set at $.3/kilometer.
   - The winning consortia would retain all revenues until they recover twice the amount of the initial investment including the cost of building and installing the trains, initial payment to government plus cost of borrowing.
   - Afterward, the consortia would share the profits (and losses) with the government.

2. A governance framework where:
   - A relationship management team comprised of representatives from the federal and provincial governments and the private sector consortia is established to manage the initiative. From a

strategic perspective, this body would act as the board of directors for the relationship and would be responsible for achieving the relationship's objectives. The formation of this team means that they would have to set and define the relationship's strategic plan to identify how the relationship members would achieve the intended results including offsets.

- An operation management team that would provide ongoing alignment of the initial set up and arrangement with a focus on creating a truly dynamic risk/reward sharing relationship as well as establish the open book financial management framework. This team would include:
  - i. A group to examine customer service
  - ii. Consumers fee schedule
  - iii. Tax holiday and rate of depreciation expense
  - iv. Cost and revenue
  - v. Business process
  - vi. Additional incentives
  - vii. A broader stakeholder's advisory board comprised of representatives of the airline industry, business leaders, and consumer groups.

QUESTION:

What are the strengths and weaknesses of this arrangement?

ANSWER:

1. Strengths:
    - Risk sharing
    - No cap on government revenue
    - Government has an ongoing say about the quality of the service and the pricing and conditions of service to support government's long-term agenda
    - Consumer protection fixed fee schedule
    - Creating a monopoly
    - Safety – governments can have an oversight function

What improvements would you recommend?

2. Weaknesses:
    - Requires a management structure that has an ongoing cost
    - Requires open financial systems and tools
    - How could it be improved?
    - Twice the initial investment may be too high of an initial ROI
    - Tax holiday may not be necessary

- An accelerated depreciation schedule would have the same effect as a tax holiday. Consider having one, not both.

This case study provides another basic example of the depth and breadth of the honest dialogue required to ensure the collaborative success of any initiative. It will be essential to establish a shared mission, and vision relationship under a Relationship Charter (whether joint or otherwise), as well as create an open book framework.

The above examples illustrate why the vendor selection process is such a critical part of the entire engagement process. (See page 44)

References

[i] Mayer, K. J., and Argyres, N. S. 2004. "Learning to Contract: Evidence from the Personal Computer Industry," Organization Science.

[ii] Poppo, L., and Zenger, T. 2002. "Do Formal Contracts and Relational Governance Function as Substitutes or Complements?," *Strategic Management Journal*

[iii] J. Hansen, Sept. 2005, "Acres of Diamonds: The Value of Effectively Managing Low-Dollar, High Transactional Spend," *Procurement Insights*

[iv] from April 24th, 2007 *Forbes* article "The Wal-Mart Squeeze" by Tom Van Riper.

[v] 'Madison Avenue ooops . . . make that Gartner, names Oracle as a leader in supply chain planning'

[vi] Reference link - http://en.wikipedia.org/wiki/Porter_five_forces_analysis

[vii] *Developing Country Firms in the World Economy: Governance and Upgrading in Global Value Chains* by John Humphrey and Hubert Schmitz, 2002

[viii] from the January 2011 paper "Building the supply chain of the future" by Yogesh Malik, Alex Niemeyer, Brian Ruwadi, *McKinsey Quarterly* (Operations Practice)

[ix] Reference link - http://en.wikipedia.org/wiki/Strategic_group

[x] Reference link - http://thechronicleherald.ca/canada/148944-irving-tries-to-keep-contract-details-secret

[xi] Reference link - http://www.thecoast.ca/RealityBites/archives/2012/12/20/will-halifax-lose-shipbuilding-work

[xii] "Strategic Analysis and Action (1986 to 2004)" by Joseph N. Fry and Peter J. Killing, Prentice Hall

[xiii] Reference link - http://thechronicleherald.ca/canada/148944- irving-tries-to-keep-contract-details-secret

[xiv] Reference link - http://en.wikipedia.org/wiki/Critical_success_factor

[xv] Reference link - http://en.wikipedia.org/wiki/Critical_success_factor

[xvi] Reference link - http://en.wikipedia.org/wiki/McKinsey_7S_Framework

[xvii] from the book *Competitive Advantage: Creating and Sustaining Superior Performance* by Michael E. Porter (1998), Free Press

[xviii] from the book *Clusters Facing Competition: The Importance of External Linkages* by Elisa Giuliani, Roberta Rabellotti, Meine Pieter van Dijk (2005), Ashgate Pub. Co.

[xix] Reference link for Raphael Kaplinsky - http://www.globalvaluechains.org/researcher_info.php?r_id=121, from the article "Value Chains An Economist's Perspective" by Adrian Wood (2001, 2009), *IDS Bulletin Wiley*

[xx] Reference link to Professor and Dean Harvey Goldstein - http://www.modul.ac.at/study-programs/post-graduate-studies/faculty-research-profiles/profiles/harvey-goldstein/

[xxi] Heakal, Reem (2003): "What Are Economies of Scale?," in Investopedia, http://www.investopedia.com/articles/03/012703.asp and, Heakal, Reem (2009): "What Are

Economies of Scale?," in Investopedia, http://www. investopedia.com/articles/03/012703.asp

[xxii] from the paper *Developing Country Firms in the World Economy: Governance and Upgrading in Global Value Chains* by John Humphrey and Hubert Schmitz, 2002

[xxiii] from the paper "THE DEVELOPMENT OF A SOFTWARE CLUSTER IN NANJING" referencing Meine Pieter van Dijk and Wang Quansheng - http://oldweb.eco.unipmn.it/eventi/eadi/ papers/vandijkquansheng.pdf

[xxiv] Reference link - http://en.wikipedia.org/wiki/Performance_ Based_Contracting

[xxv] "Utilizing an Intelligent Filtering Platform to Enhance Contract Performance" by Jon Hansen, 2009, *Procurement Insights*, http://www.slideshare.net/piblogger/utilizing-an- intelligent-filtering-platform-to-enhance-contract-performance- white-paper-1321951

[xxvi] Reference link - http://en.wikipedia.org/wiki/Formula_for_ Change

[xxvii] from the article "DoD procurement practice then and now: A public versus private sector comparison (Part 1)" by Jon Hansen, August 16th, 2007, *Procurement Insights* - http://procureinsights.wordpress.com/2007/08/16/ dod-procurement-practice-then-and-now-a-public-versus-private-sector-comparison-part-1/

[xxviii] Reference link - http://www.dau.mil/pubscats/PubsCats/ AR%20Journal/arq99/bessel.pdf

[xxix] *2013 Procurement & Strategic Sourcing Data Survey* - http://consero.com/2013-procurement-strategic-sourcing-data-survey-2/

xxx "Good To Great" by Jim Collins, Oct. 4th, 2001. *Harper Business*, Chapter 8

xxxi Reference link - http://contractiq.wordpress.com/2013/03/21/focus-on-building-relationships-that-create-sustainable-value-in-canada-key-to-cf-18-hornet-replacement-contract-part-1-by-andy-akrouche/

xxxii "Towards an international model for Canadian defence procurement? An F-35 Case Study une étude de c as sur le F-35 Vers un modèle international pour les approvisionnements de défense du Canada?" by Richard Shimooka - http://www.cdainstitute.ca/images/F-35_Case_Study.pdf

xxxiii Reference link - http://www.ic.gc.ca/eic/site/042.nsf/eng/home

xxxiv Reference link - http://en.wikipedia.org/wiki/Three-sector_hypothesis

xxxv from the white paper "Succeeding in a Dynamic World: Supply Management in the Decade Ahead" (2007) by Phillip L. Carter, DBA, Joseph R. Carter, DBA, C.P.M., Robert M. Monczka, Ph.D., C.P.M., John D. Blascovich, Thomas H. Slaight, William J. Markham - http://www.atkearneypas.com/knowledge/reports/2007/SuccDynamicFINAL10_25_07.pdf

.

www.ingramcontent.com/pod-product-compliance
Lightning Source LLC
Chambersburg PA
CBHW021035210326
41598CB00016B/1030